WE REMEMBER
C.S. LEWIS

Essays & Memoirs

WE REMEMBER
C. S. LEWIS
Essays & Memoirs

DAVID Graham [Editor]

BROADMAN
&HOLMAN
PUBLISHERS

NASHVILLE, TENNESSEE

0-8054-2299-4

Published by Broadman & Holman Publishers, Nashville, Tennessee

Dewey Decimal Classification: 230
Subject Heading: C. S. LEWIS
Library of Congress Card Catalog Number: 00-046834

Photos on the cover and pages 4, 5, and 154 are used by permission of The Marion E. Wade Center, Wheaton College, Wheaton, Illinois. Except for the three Wade collection pictures, all photographs are by Roger Stronstad unless otherwise noted.

Unless otherwise stated all Scripture citation is from the New American Standard Bible, © the Lockman Foundation, 1960, 1962, 1963, 1968, 1971, 1972, 1973, 1975, 1977; used by permission.

Library of Congress Cataloging-in-Publication Data
We remember C. S. Lewis : essays and memoirs /
      edited by David Graham.
          p.   cm.
    ISBN 0-8054-2299-4 (pbk.)
    1. Lewis, C. S. (Clive Staples), 1898–1963.
    I. Graham, David, 1963–.

BX5199.L53 W4   2001
230'.092—dc21
                                        00-046834
                                              CIP

1 2 3 4 5 6 7 8 9 10 05 04 03 02 01

CONTENTS

LECTURER

BIOGRAPHY

OUTSIDE THE CLASSROOM

PREFACE

Stephen Schofield (1915–1993) founded *The Canadian C. S. Lewis Journal* in 1979 because of the disappointment he felt from having his manuscript on C. S. Lewis rejected by a publishing firm. At the time, Macmillan Publishing Company was bringing out *C. S. Lewis at the Breakfast Table*, a book of reminiscences by almost two dozen people who knew Lewis, and such competition negated any hopes of reasonable sales for a similar book: thus the other publisher's rejection. When offers to other firms were also refused, Schofield decided to launch his journal, thinking there would be enough material to keep it going for at least a year or two. More than two decades later, the journal is still being produced, though it has changed from a monthly publication about C. S. Lewis to a biannual production about Lewis and the other six writers featured in Wheaton College's Wade Collection (George MacDonald, G. K. Chesterton, Owen Barfield, Charles Williams, Dorothy Sayers, and J. R. R. Tolkien). Schofield (whose editing chores were passed on to Roger Stronstad in 1993) was eventually satisfied with the turn of events that inaugurated the journal. He came to feel that the format of a regular periodical resulted in more important reports, letters, and diffusion of truth about Lewis than any book he could have edited. As a Christian, the Pauline doctrine, "God causes all things to work together for good to those who love God, to those who are called according to His purpose" (Rom. 8:28), would certainly reflect Schofield's feelings about the initial rejections of his Lewis manuscript for publication.

On the other hand, Ecclesiastes states that "there is an appointed time for everything," and eventually Schofield's time for publication came in 1983 when his manuscript *In Search of C. S. Lewis* was accepted and printed. It was a triumph and a disappointment. The articles and letters he had collected were varied, lively, and revealing, making the book a pleasurable reading experience for Lewis enthusiasts. Unfortunately, the publisher took a lackadaisical, slovenly approach to the project. A picture of the Ottawa Peace Tower in Canada appeared in the book with the caption "Magdalen Tower" (in Oxford, England). Small 10-point type was used instead of larger (and easier to read) 12 point. Two whole sentences of conversation were left out of one story, confusing the passage. Letters from contributors were not placed in appropriate chapter groupings, and in one case, letters from two different writers were combined into one. A large photograph of a Lewis friend Schofield had interviewed was considerably cropped and reduced. Numerous typographical errors marred the text. As Schofield himself later wrote in his article "How to Publish a Flop," "In a word it appears that a way to ensure a flop is to print a poor picture of Ottawa as Oxford opposite page one, jam letters under wrong headings, allow 26 typographical errors, use no art or glossy paper for photographs, reduce a vital photograph to the size of a postage stamp, print one article twice, use small type throughout, release review copies in the U.S. at the peak of the Christmas rush, allow only five copies in the U.K., and in the first place, refuse to print anything that 'might offend some readers.' That will be it."

Regardless of the mixed feelings about the book, interest in the journal continued. Friends, colleagues, pupils, acquaintances, and long distance admirers of Lewis contributed articles and letters, diving into lively discussions and occasional acrimonious debates.

The letters to the journal from its constituency were often as interesting as the articles that inspired them. As the years rolled by, a rich collection of articles accumulated. Although Schofield expressed his desire to publish a sequel to *In Search of C. S. Lewis*, he did not do so, partly due to ill health in his last few years. This book is the sequel that has finally been made, bringing to fruition the desire for the journal's labors to see wider exposure.

Concern has been voiced from time to time about the intensity of focus on C. S. Lewis and the hagiographical apotheosis that seems to occur in the minds of many Lewis devotees, especially in America. Isn't this the "personal heresy" that Lewis himself disapproved? Doesn't this amount to a kind of idolatry, putting the mammon of C. S. Lewis before God? Does all of the haggling about Lewis by those of opposing viewpoints represent that which the apostle Paul instructed Timothy to avoid, "worldly and empty chatter, for it will lead to further ungodliness"? Does it violate his advice to the Colossians to "set your mind on the things above, not on the things that are on earth"? Quite possibly it can, and sometimes does. Schofield's own son, Woodman, expressed such concerns to the journal, feeling that attention on Lewis detracted from what should be the focus of a Christian's faith, that of praising, worshiping, and obeying the Godhead: Father, Son, and Holy Ghost.

It is not the intention of this book to change the focus of anyone's belief away from God, nor distract readers from studying the Bible. Nor is there intent to overplay Lewis's role in Christendom, ignore his shortcomings, or inflate his status as a writer, tutor, or scholar. His written works will stand or fall on their own merits, needing no "help" from our small quarter to boost their popularity. As for the man himself, he would be the first to admit his fallibility, to being a fellow sinner with faults and weaknesses. Some of those foibles will be discussed in the pages of this book; and it is no more necessary to turn all "Lewis studies" into devotional worship than it is to do likewise with other subjects like "physics studies," "medieval literature studies," or "political science studies." Like him or dislike him, agree or disagree with him, attracted or repelled by his style, the fact remains that C. S. Lewis was a fascinating person. Wonderful novelist, unsuccessful poet, warm letter correspondent, impersonal tutor, cynical atheist, Christian apologist: Lewis was many things in his life; but he was rarely dull. The man and his writings remain enjoyable to study. Discussing even the minute details about Lewis—as Lincoln's or Shakespeare's or Jefferson's biographers do with them—is a means of interesting discovery for many readers. As Samuel Johnson (himself a Christian) once said, "There is nothing, Sir, too little for so little a creature as man. It is by studying little things that we attain the great art of having as little misery and as much happiness as possible." Taking interest in the life of someone such as Lewis in no way precludes an appropriate, reverential worship of God. While it does represent a temptation to religious distraction and hagiography if overindulged, more often than not, a study of Lewis actually enhances the spiritual life of the reader. It is with this hope that this book is published.

While discussing Hosea in the first volume of his book *The Prophets*, Abraham Joshua Heschel states, "We cannot adequately understand a person by the impressions he produces in other people." The compendium of essays comprising *We Remember C. S. Lewis* will admittedly not bring anyone to a full knowledge of C. S. Lewis. On the other hand, such an anthology can deepen our understanding of him. It can also comment and expound upon subjects that interested him, continuing to dialogue about the issues he found important. Perhaps such a volume will also encourage a wider reading of his works.

Finally, by way of reiteration, if studying C. S. Lewis merely spotlights the man, without looking at the things he himself was pointing to—God, his world, the divine gift of imagination and creativity as seen in man's literary and artistic productions, salvation through Christ—then we are simply adding to life's foundation a pile of wood, hay, and straw, which the apostle Paul assured the Corinthians would be shown for what it is on the day of judgment. C. S. Lewis is not the *object* of our highest calling, he is a *guide*—a flawed, yet fascinating and brilliant one—in our pursuit of truth and understanding. We are thankful for his example, his insight, and the enjoyment his work continues to give to each new generation of readers.

ACKNOWLEDGMENTS

The editor of *The Canadian C. S. Lewis Journal,* Roger Stronstad, coordinates and organizes the writings of the journal's many contributors, producing a fine periodical about Lewis and the other six writers featured in the Wheaton College Wade Collection—J. R. R. Tolkien, G. K. Chesterton, George MacDonald, Owen Barfield, Dorothy Sayers, and Charles Williams. His suggestions, helpful source hunting, and photographs enhanced the content of this book significantly.

Many thanks are due to all of the contributors of this book. Their willingness to share memories and insights of C. S. Lewis is deeply appreciated. Some have passed on from this life to the next since the creation of their articles, and though they are not here to receive the editor's thanks, the charitable spirit that led them to offer these pieces for publication in *The Canadian C. S. Lewis Journal* is gratefully acknowledged.

Stephen Schofield's persistent efforts to found *The Canadian C. S. Lewis Journal,* to obtain interviews and articles for it, as well as pay money out of his own pocket for investigative research on some matters, is admirable and valued. Although he is no longer living, the many people who have reaped the benefits of his hard work are grateful for his endeavors. Without him, this book would never have been conceived.

Sketch of C. S. Lewis by Juliet Pannett. This appeared on the masthead of The Canadian C. S. Lewis Journal, *#1-83.*

WHAT FRANCE MEANS TO YOU

C. S. Lewis

In the April 15, 1944, edition of the French journal LaFrance Libre: Liberte, Egalite, Fraternite, C. S. Lewis and several other contributors offered brief responses to the statement "What France Means to You." After its appearance, it quietly went the way of most magazine essays to a long repose, only to be quickened fifty years later when Kurt Berends came across it in a used book shop in Oxford, England. His rediscovery of this long-forgotten Lewis composition was an exciting experience, leading to its republication (along with an English translation) in the spring 1995 issue of The Canadian C. S. Lewis Journal. *It is here published in a book for the first time.*

On m'a demandé d'écrire quelques mots sur la France, et plus particulièrement sur son avenir. Des circonstances futures, nous ne savons rien; et nous ne pouvons imaginer l'avenir d'un être vivant que d'après son passé et son présent. Ce qui me conduit à me

I have been asked to write a few words about France, and more particularly about its future. Of future circumstances, we know nothing; and we can imagine the future of a living being only on the basis of its past and its present. Which leads me to wonder

demander ce que la France a été pour l'homme. Inévitablement, je pense d'abord à la France médiévale: car c'est au moyen âge que votre nation a exercé sur l'Europe une hégémonie spirituelle que ni elle, ni aucune autre nation, n'a égalée depuis lors. Avant tout, la France représente les Croisades, la Chanson de Roland, la cathédrale de Chartres, le Cycle d'Arthur, l'Université de Paris. Dans tout cela, ce qui frappe, c'est l'éclat: éclat des épées, de la courtoisie, de la logique. En second lieu, je pense à la France "éclairée", celle de Voltaire et des Encyclopédistes. L'éclat en a pâli, mais la clarté demeure. Cette France-là, je la considère un peu comme mon ennemie, mais c'est une noble ennemie; à défaut d'amour, elle m'inspire du respect. Enfin, pour être tout à fait franc avec vous, je pense à une troisième France, celle où les pires cancers du monde moderne ont trouvé leur climat d'élection, celle où adorent flâner les Américains décadents, celle où Edgar Poë passe pour un grand poète, celle des petits "movements" vermiculaires, du Dadaïsme, du Surréalisme et

what France has meant for humanity. Inevitably, I think first of all of medieval France: since it was in the Middle Ages that your nation exerted a spiritual hegemony over Europe which neither she, nor any other nation, has equalled since. Above all, France means the Crusades, the Song of Roland, Chartres Cathedral, the Arthurian cycle, the University of Paris. In all that, what is most striking is brilliance: the brilliant flash of swords, of courtliness, of logic. Secondly, I think of "enlightened" France, Voltaire's and the Encyclopedists'. The brilliance has faded, but clarity remains. That France, I consider a little as my enemy, but it is a noble one; it inspires respect on my part, if not love. Finally to be perfectly frank with you, I also think of a third France, the one where the worst cancers of the modern world have chosen to take up residence, the one where decadent Americans love to stroll, the one where Edgar Poe passes for a great poet, that of the little, slithery "movements," dadaism, surrealism,

des Messes Noires—celle qui au pays même de la Raison a dressé l'idole de la Betise. Il semble que votre être soit double. Sans doute en est-il de même de toutes les nations; je vois qu'il en est de même de mon pays. Derrière l'Angleterre de Sidney, je distingue (hélas!) celle de Cecil Rhodes. Si l'une affranchit les esclaves, l'autre s'engraisse à faire la traite. Nous qui avons failli inventer la Liberté avons aussi péché contre elle plus que presque toute autre nation. Pour vous comme pour nous, le Démon est véritablement l'envers de l'être authentique; il incite les concitoyens de Shelley à la Tyrannie, comme ceux d'Abélard à la Bêtise. L'avenir dépend, pour chacun de nos deux pays, du choix que nous ferons entre notre bon et notre mauvais génie. Est-il trop tard pour retrouver cette autre France, cette autre Angleterre?

Pour les retrouver, il ne suffit pas d'y penser. Ce n'est pas d' "idéal" ni d' "inspiration" que nous avons besoin, mais de simple probité, de charité, de diligence, pour faire face successivement à toutes les tâches

and Satanic masses—the one where even in the country of Reason the idol of Stupidity has been raised. It seems that your being is double. No doubt it's the same with all nations; I note that it is the same in my own country. Behind Sidney's England, I can see (unfortunately!) that of Cecil Rhodes. If the one frees slaves, the other gets fat by trading in them. We who have almost invented liberty have also sinned against her more than almost any other nation. For you as for us, the Devil is truly the obverse of our authentic being; he incites Shelley's citizens to Tyranny, as he incites Abelard's to Stupidity. The future depends, for each of our two countries, on the choice we make between our good and our evil genius. Is it too late to find that other France, that other England?

If we are going to find them, it won't be enough just to think about it. It's not "ideal" nor "inspiration" that we need, but simple probity, charity, perseverance, in order to face one by one all the tasks which will arise. I do not know

qui s'imposeront. Je ne sais si les Français ou les Anglais, ou les Allemands (qui, eux non plus, n'ont pas toujours connu le sul Démon) parviendront à redevenir eux-mêmes. Le salut d'un peuple, comme celui d'un individu, est toujours possible, mais aussi impossible à prédire; car nous avons des volontés libres, et l'avenir reste à faire.

whether the French or the English, or the Germans (who have also had to face more than the one Devil) will succeed in becoming themselves again. The salvation of a people, like that of an individual, is always possible, but also impossible to predict; for we have free will, and the future remains to be made.

C. S. Lewis at home in a familiar activity: writing.

Lewis, with walking stick, outside an English country church in 1938. He took great pleasure in such countryside rambles.

WHAT LEWIS WAS AND WASN'T

J. I. Packer

Dr. James I. Packer was born in Gloucestershire, England, in 1926 and educated at Oxford University (degrees in classics and theology; D.Phil. 1954). Ordained in 1952, he has served at several churches, seminaries, study centers, and colleges, taking on roles as assistant minister, seminary tutor, warden, principal, as well as associate principal. In 1979 he became Professor of Systematic and Historical Theology at Regent College, Vancouver, Canada, where in 1989 he was installed as the first Sangwoo Youtong Chee Professor of Theology. Since 1996 he has been Board of Governors Professor of Theology. He is widely known throughout Christendom for his writing and lecturing, having written numerous books and articles for various publications, including Fundamentalism and the Word of God, A Passion for Faithfulness, Rediscovering Holiness, Knowing and Doing God's Will, *and* Truth and Power, *among many others. Out of all his books, the best-seller* Knowing God *may well be the title most people think of when they hear the name J. I. Packer. This article was originally written for the magazine* Christianity Today, *January 15, 1988, and is reprinted, slightly modified, with permission.*

Americans, hearing that I am an Oxford man, often ask me if I knew C. S. Lewis, and their faces fall when I say no. American interest in Lewis, who died thirty-five years ago never having visited America, staggers me. Writing about him is a growth industry (and some of Lewis's own books still sell by the thousands); he is the star of the Wade Collection at Wheaton College (Illinois); Christian institutions mount courses on him; and Washington, D.C., has an academic unit called the C. S. Lewis Institute. Yet do North Americans see clearly the Lewis on whom they gaze? I wonder.

When I say I did not know him, I mean I had no personal link with him. (Nor did most of his pupils; they found him an awesome academic who hid his sensitive heart behind a debater's façade of urbane, loud-voiced pugnacity. "I'm a butcher, a rough and brutal man," he told one of them.) I heard him speak once, on the medievalism of the Anglican theologian Richard Hooker. He was supposed to be the best lecturer in Oxford, and on that showing it could have been true, though in the Oxford of my day the compliment meant less than you might think.

I have been a Lewis reader for over fifty years. As an unbeliever, I enjoyed *Screwtape Letters* and *Mere Christianity* more for their manner than for their matter, for Lewis's writing style made him seem both a fellow schoolboy and a wise old uncle simultaneously, and that was fascinating. His subsequent Christian essays, which I read after conversion, seemed less schoolboyish and more grandfatherly; but maybe the change was more in me than in him. His supreme achievement, for my money, is the stark and stunning *Pilgrim's Regress*, his first apologetic book, which I reread for pleasure as often, I guess, as I do Bunyan's allegory that inspired it.

Lewis's fiction thrills me less, due to its lapses from the admirably adult to the archly adolescent, and from the childlike to the childish. His no-nonsense, midtwentieth-century way with words served a late-Victorian imagination streaked with sentimentality, and the results were uneven. *Perelandra* (Eden replayed, with a different outcome) and Aslan in the Narnia books are surely Lewis's best fictional achievements. *Till We Have Faces* is more perfect as art but less powerful as vision, while *That Hideous Strength*, despite its fine title, is (to my mind, anyway) hideously bad.

His brand of Christianity was conservative Anglicanism with "catholic" (non-Roman!) leanings; hence his nonpenal view of the Atonement, his nonmention of justification, his belief in purgatory, his praying for the dead, and his regular confession to his priest. His conversion was a return to a boyhood faith lost two decades before.

Like other Oxbridge dons, he was something of a high-minded eccentric. The quixotic chivalry with which he housed the mother of a dead friend for thirty years and then married a Jewish Christian divorcee on what appeared to be her deathbed, plus (going from the near sublime to the near ridiculous) his resolute refusal to read newspapers, equally show this.

Like other Ulstermen, he loved verbal battles in which he could challenge the conventional and upset apple carts. This is as clear in his professional writing as literary critic and historian of ideas as in his joyous reassertion of old original Christianity against its detractors.

He loved beer, too, though he was rarely ever drunk.

A standard-issue evangelical? Hardly. But he was a Christian thinker and communicator without peer on three themes: the reasonableness and humanity of Christian faith; the moral demands of discipleship; and heaven as *home*, the place of all value and all contentment. The vivid way in which Lewis, who was something of a homeless child all his life, projects this vision in *The Voyage of the Dawn Treader*, *The Last Battle* (last page), and *The Great Divorce* verifies utterly the fundamental formula of communication: that reason plus imagination, tuned together, equals power. The wisdom and greatness of Lewis may—indeed, must—be measured by moments like these.

Thank you, Mr. Lewis, for being you. I wouldn't have missed you for the world.

NARNIA: THE DOMAIN OF LEWIS'S BELIEFS

M. A. Manzalaoui

Many people have written commentaries about C. S. Lewis's
Chronicles of Narnia, *including Clyde Kilby's helpful insights in*
The Christian World of C. S. Lewis, Kathryn Lindskoog's The
Lion of Judah in Never-Never Land, Evan K. Gibson's C. S.
Lewis: Spinner of Tales, *and Paul Ford's encyclopedia,*
Companion to Narnia. *Here, M. A. Manzalaoui, formerly pro-
fessor of English at the University of British Columbia in
Vancouver, Canada, shares some of his insights as a former Lewis
pupil coming from a Middle Eastern background. Professor
Manzalaoui was a pupil of C. S. Lewis from 1945–1948, writing
his Oxford B. Litt. thesis on eighteenth-century English translations from Arabic. He has written articles on Chaucer, courtly
love in Medieval Western and Arabic literature, Lewis, and modern English fiction concerned with Egypt. He has also edited*
Arabic Writings Today, *volumes 1 and 2 (1968, 1977).*

C. S. Lewis's students were taken by surprise when he published
The Lion, the Witch and the Wardrobe late in 1950, in time for the
Christmas-present trade. Since the twenties, Lewis had published
poetry, religious books, and critical and historical works concerning English literature, including a groundbreaking work on

medieval allegorical love literature. He had been an outstanding lecturer and tutor in English Literature, in philosophy, and political theory. But none of us associated this bachelor don with any interest in children.

The indications, however, were there for people to notice. He had already written science fiction—another form of fantasy. He was known to be a friend and associate of J. R. R. Tolkien, who had published *The Hobbit* before the war. He was interested in non-realistic fiction. Further reasons for turning to children's fantasies are given by Lewis himself in his critical essays: principally he writes with typical common sense that sometimes "a children's story is the best art form for something you have to say."

Of this method he says that there came into his mind the picture of Mr. Tumnus in the woods, or rather, of a faun—the classical deity with horns and tails—carrying parcels and an umbrella. Other pictures followed spontaneously. Then the pictures joined up to form a story—rather, I suppose—like pictures in a comic strip cartoon. But where gaps remained, his deliberate inventing had to come into play. The personality of the adult writer and of the child who is conceived of as the reader came together to create a composite personality which produces the book.

Of the content he writes that non-human characters present human "types" more succinctly than realistic ones, implying that non-realism can, so to speak, be more successfully true to life than realism: "As for the genre of the fairy tale, it can add to one's perception of the actual world a new dimension, that of depth." Given all this, one cannot neglect in addition the considerable influence of Tolkien's essay, "On Fairy-Stories," to which we shall come towards the end of this essay. Lewis insists on our not treating the story merely as surface, concealing and *meaning* something else. Further meaning than the immediate is there, but not to be dug out by a process that scratches out the surface meaning and forms an intellectual puzzle. In other words, we are not dealing with an allegory or an imitation of truth, but the creating of a secondary world which works upon us by our enjoying it for its own sake.

It might be thought that as a scholar of medieval allegory, Lewis set out to create continuous, consistent, and strict allegory here, but he has not.[1] I believe that there is occasional allegory here, and it occurs at important points in the narrative. The chief points are the following: First, in the concluding Narnian book, *The Last Battle*, the final and glorious apocalypse in which cosmic Narnia is destroyed and reborn as the supernal Narnia: a fairy-tale version of chapters 14 through 22 of the *Book of Revelation*. Secondly, at the climax of *The Lion, the Witch and the Wardrobe*, the Atonement for Edmund's treachery by Aslan, Aslan's Dejection, the Stations of his ordeal, his slaying, the visit of the women, or rather, the two girls, to his resting place and his Resurrection. This is so close to the biblical accounts that it is astonishing to learn from Lewis himself that there are readers who failed to see the connection with the Crucifixion and the Resurrection. I can testify as a fact that the widow of a colleague of mine said to me that she couldn't recall anything particularly Christian about *The Lion, the Witch and the Wardrobe*.

It is true, nevertheless, that the general method of the *Chronicles of Narnia* is not allegory—not loose allegory, and emphatically not the strict allegory of the medievals and of Spenser, with its layers of fourfold meaning. Perhaps some term such as *transposition, similitude,* or *counterpart* could be used for those elements in the Narnia stories which have a symbolic meaning—or one could use Dorothy L. Sayer's term *symbolic image*, which she uses for those of the features of Dante's *Divine Comedy* which are not allegorical. I stress this, because a search for allegorical meaning in every detail of Lewis's stories will lead one wildly astray—just as the attempt to impose strict and continuous allegory upon the New Testament parables breaks down; to accept that, you would have to believe that Jesus Christ thought it sinful not to wear evening dress at formal party, and thought it wrong not to invest one's friend's money in the Stock Market, a conclusion we will reach if we misread the Parable of the Wedding Feast and the Parable of the Talents. Another reason for stressing the point is to caution against a present-day tendency to employ the word *allegory* for every use of features in any way remotely symbolic, to look for a skeletal program behind a story or poem, and ignore the work of art itself, and the width of the range of different forms of symbolism.

Let us note in this connection that Lewis wrote, "Let pictures tell their own moral. It'll rise from spiritual roots you have succeeded in striking during the whole course of your life."

It is clear from Lewis's essay, "On Writing for Children," that he set out on a double task: to treat child readers as the personalities and interests of children require, but never to patronize a child-reader, a particularly difficult task for a bachelor university teacher whose contact with children was not close. He jokes in this same essay about Arthur Mee, the editor of the *Children's Encyclopedia* and *Children's Newspaper*, under whose weight of writings I myself suffered for much of my boyhood, that he has "been told that Arthur Mee never met a child and never wished to." It seems to me that Lewis succeeds in his stories because he is speaking to the child that he remembers having been. This, by the way, is combined in *The Lion, The Witch, and the Wardrobe* with Lewis also representing his own views, and those of his friend Charles Williams, in the character of the Professor—the grown-up who understands the veracity and the importance for the children of having had their everyday life traversed by an experience of the beyond. If you have only read the first of the *Narnia Chronicles*, it will not be clear to you that the story grows more profound as it develops, as a study of human spiritual growth, and of the position of humankind in relation to the universe and to God.

That is a grandiose claim to make for a series of seven children's stories. So it may be as well, before proceeding further, to mention some of the faults and limitations of the Narnia books. A North American reader in the new millennium will notice that the stories are firmly set in Britain during and immediately after the Second World War. The Pevensie children are staying at the Professor's (as children had stayed in Lewis's household) because of the arrangement made, just before the outbreak of war, to evacuate children from threatened cities to safe havens. The reader is expected to understand how small Lucy's handkerchief is found by Giant Rumblebuffin by being told it was only about the same size to him that a saccharine tablet would be to you—a familiarity brought about, not by attempts to slim, but by sugar rationing. This is not blameworthy, but the firmly genteel and upper-middle-class perspective may be found irritating. In *Prince Caspian* we read "whatever hot-houses you people may have, you have never tasted such grapes"; in *The Magician's Nephew*, Lewis himself sounds like his airhead character Lasaraleen of *The Horse and His Boy* when he jauntily says, "Everyone had lots of servants in those days." There are inconsistencies between one book and another as to who were the first earthlings to reach Narnia; an inconsistency can be found within a tale: the Witch is unfamiliar with the door to the world of man at one point in *The Lion, the Witch, and the Wardrobe*: five pages later she shows she is familiar with it. Finally, am I alone among readers of *The Dawn Treader* in finding the treatment of the one-legged Dufflepuds rather callous, reduced as they are to hopping about on a single leg as a penalty for their stupidity, and for the amusement of others?[2]

More seriously, in *The Horse and His Boy*, the pseudo-oriental nation of the Calormenes is shown as having an unpleasant religion, an invented one, but one which in many ways is a parody of features taken from Hinduism, Islam, and the religion of the ancient Canaanites, and they have a culture resembling the Indian and Middle Eastern cultures. Although the Calormenes are given some good qualities, they have unattractive traits based on the personal habits of less respectable Middle Easterners—for instance, they smell "of garlic and onions." Here I must plead a personal reaction, since this is a hostile Western view of my own cultural background. It is true, however, that this view is counterbalanced in *The Last Battle* by an important theological act of latitude which I wish to come back to. Notice, nevertheless, the quite unfair stress on the power rather than the mercy of the Calormene god Tash. Lewis takes the Moslem invocation "in the name of God, the *compassionate*, the *merciful*," and turns it into the Calormene formula, "In the name of Tash, the *irresistible*, the *inexorable*."[3]

But it is time to turn to more positive points. Let us note now the basic governing pattern of every one of the Narnia stories— closeness of the supernatural, the divine, to the mundane, the everyday, the humdrum. The normal pattern in a Narnia story is for a number of children to be whisked out of their ordinary lives, to find themselves voluntarily taking part in a quest with a very serious and lofty purpose, in which their spiritual growth is an outstanding factor. In some cases, a child who is gravely guilty— such as Edmund in *The Lion, The Witch, and the Wardrobe*— reforms and becomes heroic. The children meet Aslan at important junctures in the quest, and have a closer encounter with him at the conclusion. I cannot tell if the episodic meetings, the warnings and guidance of Aslan, are meant to be a parallel to prevenient grace, while the climactic meetings are analogues to what is called "efficacious" grace, but the conclusion of *The Last Battle* certainly parallels the Beatific Vision granted to the redeemed. In terms of the art of story-telling, the narrative itself in the same way proceeds from level to level of dignity. Early in the story there is cosy homeliness: the wardrobe in the Professor's house on earth, Mr. Tumnus' tea and sardines on toast, Mrs. Beaver with her sewing-machine, her fried trout and boiled potatoes; in the middle of the book there is a deal of romantic questing: Edmund's entry into the Witch's House, the sight of the animals that have been turned to stone, the children's trek through the wilds as the age-old winter breaks resplendently into spring. Then comes the battle of Cair Paravel, and finally we move from the heroics of that fight to the spiritual battle of the submission, death, and resurrection of Aslan. In the same way, published over a decade before Lewis's first sketching of the plan of *The Lion, The Witch, and the Wardrobe*, Tolkien's *The Hobbit* proceeds from the domestic to the romantic and on to the epic, from Hobbiton to the Misty Mountains and Mirkwood, and on to the Battle of the Five Armies—though, in its case, there is no openly spiritual development. To keep the child reader anchored to everyday life, however highflying the spiritual adventures become, there are the ordinary objects which play important roles in the stories—the wardrobe as the gateway to Narnia, the London street lamppost which is growing in the woods in Narnia (and, by the way, I claim to know the earthly origins of this object).[4] Domestic imagery is also involved in some of the similes and reflections; so in *The Silver Chair* we have helpful references to the sounds of a vacuum cleaner and of an old-fashioned radio as it warms up, and to the feel of the second half of morning school, after break. Most striking, in returning us to the everyday, is the closing sentence of *Prince Caspian*, Edmund's remark when he finds himself back in an English railway station, "Bother! I've left my new torch in Narnia." And throughout, to produce comedy and poetry, there is the common technique of the use of fantasies by which the ordinary world and the secondary world are seen in double vision. So, in *The Silver Chair*, a younger owl says that he expects the wise old Glumfeather to say, "You're a mere chick. I remember you when you were an egg. Don't come trying to teach *me*, Sir." And in *Prince Caspian* we learn that talking trees have a varied menu of soils and waters, "rich brown loam . . . like chocolate," "a chalky soil" at the cheese stage of a meal, for a sweet "the finest gravels powdered with choice silver sand." And a centaur satisfies his human stomach with a meal like ours, and his second stomach, the horse one, with fresh grass. This is the pseudorealism of fantasy, the realism of presentation, as distinct from the realism of content. But unreal fantasies as the *Narnia Chronicles* are, they demonstrate a clear understanding of human psychology, as telling as the symbolic entities and the metaphysical truths. The children, heroic at their best, are often frightened and sometimes quarrel and are bad tempered. We recognize the joyless nonbeliever's puritanism in the Witch's complaint against partying: "What is the meaning of all this gluttony, this waste, this self-indulgence?" And we can all recognize our own responses in reflections like these: "Children have one kind of silliness . . . and grown-ups have another kind." Or: "One usually gets on better with people when one is making plans than when one is talking about nothing in particular." Or (of seeing the wicked but mortal Uncle Andrew together with the diabolical witch Jadis): "One good thing about seeing the two together was that you would never again be afraid of Uncle Andrew, any more than you'd be afraid of a worm after you had met a rattlesnake or afraid of a cow after you had met a mad bull."

As a retired professor who is attempting to continue with academic productiveness, I found one remark most relevant of all— it's about emancipation from slavery: "One of the worst results of being a slave and being forced to do things is that when there is no one to force you any more you find you have almost lost the power of forcing yourself."

In fact, Lewis is never far from his own everyday life in the Narnia books. The loyal but grumpy Puddleglum the Marshwiggle, a character in *The Silver Chair*, is based on his own gardener Paxford. But there is another source that provided a large number of details to the Narnia tales, and that is the canon of traditional literature which Lewis also lived in, as reader and as teacher. Some details are significant, others are marginal and playful, but all serve the important purpose of setting the Chronicles in a self-invigorating tradition of mainly European imaginative works. In *The Voyage of the Dawn Treader,* Aslan appears in the form of a lamb, and provides fish broiling on a fire, "the most delicious food (the children) had ever tasted." In *The Lion, The Witch, and the Wardrobe,* Aslan provides the huge crowd of revivified statues with "a fine high tea at about eight o'clock." The Gospel parallels are obvious there and important. But elsewhere, sometimes only in details of imagery, language, or passing incident, I find the following mixed bag of sources: Homer, Plato, Virgil, *The Arabian Nights, Beowulf,* the Middle English romances of *Sir Orfeo, Sir Gawain,* and *Havelock,* Malory's *Morte d'Arthur,* at least three of Chaucer's poems, Dante, Shakespeare, Milton, Wagner, *Alice in Wonderland, Huckleberry Finn,* Richmond Cromptom's *William,* and Lewis's own friends Charles Williams and Tolkien.[5]

There is one model which is more integral to the pattern of the Narnia stories, and to their theology. And that is Edmund Spenser's *Faery Queene*. In each of the six completed books of this romance epic, a hero undertakes a chivalric quest, for the good of others, and, growing in heroic and in spiritual stature, he achieves a great deal through his own effort. But at the true crisis of the tale, faced with the full power of evil, the hero cannot succeed on his own. To complete the quest, Prince Arthur intervenes, and rescues the hero, and causes his efforts to come to a happy conclusion. For the purposes of this function, Arthur can be recognized as the allegorical figure of faith, of grace, or of the Redeemer, taking over where human will and initiative are beyond being of any avail. Similarly, in the *Narnia Chronicles*, the heroes' growth, their initiative, are essential to the solution, and they are left to their own devices by Aslan, until the moment which he was waited for, when he intervenes: good works, and then grace. Notice, by the way, that in Tolkien's *The Lord of the Rings*, never far from Lewis's mind, Frodo, who has heroically set out to destroy the One Ring, when he eventually, after countless achievements, reaches the Cracks of Doom, doesn't throw the ring down. He is tempted to keep it and put its power to selfish use. It is Gollum's attempt to seize it— Gollum unknowingly being used by a power never mentioned by Tolkien—which sends it down the Cracks, to its destruction.

With this point, we are at the heart of the theology of the Narnia books. A human being is forced by his good nature into a vocation he never expected to adopt, he conquers fear, he perseveres, he grows in ability, determination, and courage, but he often fails—yet there is virtue in such failure, and it brings about the intervention of grace—Aslan, as Lewis says, comes bounding in. In fact, the virtuous actions were all along really the actions of Aslan; as Mr. Beaver says to the children, "It is he, not you, that will save Mr. Tumnus." Fortune is all providence: the Hermit in *The Horse and His Boy* says, "Daughter . . . I have now lived a hundred and nine winters in this world and have never yet met any such thing as Luck." The development of the child heroes is, of course, not as straightforward as a rapid summary suggests. Edmund is greedy and a traitor, jealous of his elder brother, eager for kingship and Turkish delight, but an early sign of his conversion comes when he sees the creatures that have been turned to stone and "for the first time in this story" feels "sorry for someone besides himself." In a later story, Eustace goes through a similar conversion. The characters who are predominantly good undergo temptation, and are blameworthy: Peter excuses Edmund to Aslan when he confesses that it was because he, Peter, had shown Edmund that he was angry with him, that he "helped him go wrong"—Peter's recognition of his own wrong action in its turn helps Peter towards self-purifying. In *The Voyage of the Dawn Treader*, Caspian and Edmund are tempted by the black magic of Deathwater Island, and fall into quarrel which stops when Aslan glides across the hillside above them. In the Edwardian flashback which is *The Magician's Nephew*, the boy Digory Kirke, whom we know in the 1940s in *The Lion, The Witch, and the Wardrobe* as the aged Professor, restrains himself from eating the apple of life, and takes it back to earth to save his mother's life, and to plant the seeds of the tree from which the Wardrobe is going to be made. In *The Horse and His Boy*, Aravis cannot escape receiving scratches from the Lion's own claws on her back, "equal to the stripes" received by "her stepmother's slave because of the drugged sleep Aravis cast upon her as part of her successful plan to escape from Calormen." Sadly, Susan falls away altogether, into grown-up vanity, and is not granted the happiness that follows for the others after they are killed in a railway crash. (Though one can hope that in years to come she will be reconverted.)[6]

It is fitting in children's literature with metaphysical implications that the sins of the main characters should be this blend of outwardly slight peccadillos and deeper sins. The same blend is found in the Narnian equivalent of human intimacy with God. Lucy and Susan romp with Aslan and snuggle into his mane, and have him tossing them into the air and catching them in his paws, but "whether it was more like playing with a thunderstorm or playing with a kitten Lucy could never make up her mind." A mixture of the awesome and the joyful is the constant characteristic of the Aslan-experience, the Narnian form of that inward act of enlightenment which is a recurrent theme in Lewis's writings, and which he calls "numinous awe": the loving and joyful fear of the protective power of God. Mr. and Mrs. Beaver try to explain the paradox to the Pevensie children:

(Susan) "Is he—quite safe? I shall feel rather nervous about meeting a lion." "That you will, dearie, and no mistake," said Mrs. Beaver; "if there's anyone who can appear before Aslan without their knees knocking, they're either braver than most or else just silly." "Then he isn't safe?" said Lucy. "Safe?" said Mr. Beaver; "don't you hear what Mrs. Beaver tells you? Who said anything about safe? 'Course he isn't safe. But he's good. He's the King, I tell you." "I'm longing to see him," said Peter, "even if I do feel frightened when it comes to the point."

Lewis had read Kenneth Grahame's *The Wind in the Willows* as an adult and he must have recognized in it his own feeling, which he describes in his autobiography, when he read of Ratty and Mole's encounter with the god Pan as he played his pipes over the strayed and sleeping otter child. In the Narnia books, no passage is more famous than the one in *The Silver Chair* in which Jill meets Aslan for the first time. Very thirsty, she has come to a stream, but finds a talking Lion lying in her way:

And the thirst became so bad that she almost
felt she would not mind being eaten by the Lion if
only she could be sure of getting a mouthful of
water first. "If you're thirsty, you may drink." . . .
The voice said again, "If you are thirsty, come and
drink." . . . The voice was not like a man's. It was
deeper, wilder, and stronger; a sort of heavy, golden
voice. It did not make her any less frightened than
she had been before, but it made her frightened in
rather a different way. "Are you not thirsty?" said
the Lion. "I'm *dying* of thirst," said Jill. "Then

drink," said the Lion. "May I—Could I—would you
mind going away while I do?" said Jill. The Lion
answered this only by a look and a very low growl.
And as Jill gazed at its motionless bulk, she realized
that she might as well have asked the whole moun-
tain to move aside for her convenience. . . . "Will
you promise not to—do anything to me, if I do
come?" said Jill. "I make no promise," said the Lion.
Jill was so thirsty now that, without noticing it, she
had come a step nearer. "*Do* you eat girls?" she said.
"I have swallowed up girls and boys, men and
women, kings and emperors, cities and realms," said
the Lion. It didn't say this as if it were boasting, nor
as if it were sorry, nor as if it were angry. It just said
it. "I daren't come and drink," said Jill. "Then you
will die of thirst," said the Lion. "Oh dear!" said Jill,
coming another step nearer. "I suppose I must go
and look for another stream then." "There is no
other stream," said the Lion. It never occurred to Jill
to disbelieve the Lion—no one who had seen his
stern face could do that—and her mind suddenly
made itself up. It was the worst thing she had ever
had to do, but she went forward to the stream and
knelt down, and began scooping up water in her
hand. It was the coldest, most refreshing water she
had ever tasted. You didn't need to drink much of
it, for it quenched your thirst at once.

There is another important passage concerning Aslan in *The
Horse and His Boy*. Two talking horses and a girl discuss the
Lionhood of Aslan, and whether this is to be believed in literally.
The Lionhood is the Narnian equivalent of the personhood of God
the Father and also of the Human nature of God the Son: like any
nontheist on our earth, Bree is the self-confident matter-of-fact
horse who swears by the Lion, merely as a figure of speech, and is

shocked that anyone should take Aslan to be a real lion. In his lecturer's voice, Bree explains condescendingly that "to speak of him as a Lion . . . only mean(s) he's as strong as a lion . . . it would be absurd and disrespectful to suppose he is a real Lion." Bree soon apologizes to Aslan when he is actually tickled in the ear by the Lion's whiskers, "Aslan . . . I'm afraid I must be rather a fool"—and this elicits the reply "Happy the Horse who knows that while he is still young. Or the Human either." (I should add that I myself am uncomfortable with the response of the humbly believing mare Hwin, which is, "Please . . . you're so beautiful. You may eat me if you like. I'd sooner be eaten by you than fed by anyone else.")

While the Lion is the pivotal symbol around which everything turns in all seven books, in the closing chapters of *The Last Battle* a stable in a field becomes the equivalent of the world beyond. Entering the stable is entering supernal life. To nonbelievers and to evil persons who enter it, it remains a small, dark, and noisome place. To those who attain salvation, it contains a vast world for, in a mystic paradox, "its inside is greater than its outside." For them the inside not only contains the Real Narnia, but beyond and above that again, a further land of Narnian happiness. (Only one critic whom I have read has noticed this doubling of heavenly archetypes, which, I confess, leaves me puzzled.) It is just as we reach the apocalyptic description of the afterlife that the topic of non-Christian religions reappears. The Calormene religion has been condemned earlier as false and diabolic: Tash, its god, is a devil who has imposed himself as a god, and the Calormenes kill men as sacrifices on his altar. Now we meet a good young Calormene, Emeth—the word is the Hebrew for *faithful* or true— who is saved because the worship he has been offering to Tash is totally pure and, without knowing it, is seeking for Aslan. "Beloved," says Aslan, "unless thy desire had been for me thou wouldst not have sought so long and so truly. For all find what they truly seek." Concomitantly, an Aslan-worshiper whose devotion takes evil forms will have performed no true devotion: "no service which is vile," says the Lion, "can be done to me." So does this positive form of ecumenism countermand the negative one which I discussed earlier?[7]

There is before us now the business of testing Lewis's own critical writing to judge how his fantasies for children fitted into his model of the interrelationship between faith, literature, and life in the world. Some impressions can be gained from his magazine article on writing for children, his book *An Experiment in Criticism*, and a paper of his which, for reasons explained in it, is surrealistically called "Bluspells and Flalansferes." To sum up his views succinctly: Imagination is as important an organ of investigation as reason is: as he writes, "Reason is the natural organ of truth; but imagination is the organ of meaning." With imagination, we create art and literature; especially, we create story, and story transmits truth. The Lewis scholar Paul Ford writes: "Lewis saw the story as a bridge between two ways of knowing reality: thinking about it and experiencing it. Thinking is incurably abstract; experiencing is always concrete." Fantasy, if used improperly, can become delusion or, as Lewis puts it, Morbid Castle-Building; to entertain it wrongly and incessantly is to injure oneself. But fantasy rightly used leads, at the least, to recreation through *normal* castle-building. But this too has its dangers, for you may dabble in it egoistically, making yourself the hero, giving yourself imaginary triumphs. Use it without this self-centredness and you will obtain healthy recreation; pass further on, and it leads you to literary invention. This informs you of Truth, and will be found to be the antechamber that opens on to Faith. This happens through the writer's creating a subordinate world of his own: Lewis sees this as more conducive to truth than the program normally accepted by modern writers, which is to create a "comment upon life."

So much for Lewis's own theoretical statements. But, oddly enough, I believe that we can learn more about the abstract underpinning of the Narnia stories by making a similar summing up of the ideas of another man, and that is his friend Tolkien. In 1946 Lewis put together a collection of essays as a memorial volume for his friend Charles Williams: the essays were by different persons, all friends of the dead writer. One of the contributions was a long and weighty one by Tolkien, with the title, "On Fairy Stories." It seems without doubt that Lewis was influenced by this essay both in his own expressed views on fantasy stories, and in the Narnia stories themselves. Let me try to sum up Tolkien's theories in this regard.

Tolkien defends Fantasy, by saying that it is not opposed to Reason; the keener the Reason, the better the Fantasy. Without the wish or the ability to see Truth, Fantasy languishes and turns into Morbid Delusion. There is no essential link between fairy tale and children; it is not true that children's credulity and their lack of experience make fairy tales suitable fare for them. It is true, however, that the child reader finds important the question of Right and Wrong. It is also true that fairy tales share elements with Myth. Man is a Subcreator and onto natural objects he imprints Personality. Fairy-Story has three Faces. The Mystical Face looks towards the Supernatural. The Magical looks towards Nature. The one Tolkien calls the "Mirror of scorn and pity" looks towards Man. In writing Fantasy the artist, as a Subcreator, uses his Will and makes a Secondary World, and that world has its rules which things in it must follow. We make Fantasy in our measure "because we are made" and "made in the image and likeness of a Maker." The art produced by our imagination, if imagination is combined with Wonder, produces Fantasy. Very debatably in my opinion, Tolkien seems to take all Fantasy to be a higher form than realism—does that mean that *The Hobbit* is a greater work than, say, Tolstoy's *War and Peace?* Now, fantasy may take different forms: strict and loose allegory are two forms; another is appreciative fantasy, in which the secondary world is enjoyed for its own sake. Another is what has been called illustrative fantasy. This seems to be the form of the Narnia stories, for enjoyable though their world is for its own sake, in them a secondary world is used to make a point about the primary world. Fantasy has three purposes. The first is Recovery: an experience of the Secondary World which restores us and refreshes our view of our Primary World. This seems to be the factor which Lewis describes as Renewal, an *"excursion into the preposterous which strengthens our relish for real life."* The second factor is Escape: here Escape is used in a positive sense and not as we normally use the word *escapism.* It is the Escape of a Prisoner, not the Flight of a Deserter. Escape satisfies desires unrealized in the Primary World. Third comes Consolation, described as an Escape from Death. It is the Consolation of the Happy Ending, the ending for which Tolkien makes up the word *Eucatastrophe* (from the Greek for "good" and "turning away"). Tolkien in this sees a happy ending as an essential of the fairy tale; speaking of the Turn, as he calls those developments which lead up to the eucatastrophe, he says that it "reflects a glory backwards," giving a joy that transcends the event in the narrative. It seems to me that Lewis in writing the last chapter of *The Last Battle* has done precisely that, giving fresh and transcending meaning to the human experience earlier in that book and in all the books that have gone before, and turning death in a railway accident, and defeat by an invading army, into freedom and happiness. Tolkien's own words, written some ten years before the final Narnia tale, succeed marvellously in encapsulating its meaning. The words have both a theological and a literary importance. Theologically, they are a justification of the use of the Art of Comedy to convey spiritual truth. As literary criticism, they give to Comedy something of the deep and important status normally given only to Tragedy. The passage is the following: "It (Eucatastrophe) does not deny the existence of *dyscatastrophe*, of sorrow and failure: the possibility of these is necessary to the joy of deliverance; it denies (in the face of much evidence, if you will) universal final defeat and insofar is *evangelium*, giving a fleeting glimpse of Joy, Joy beyond the walls of the world, poignant as grief."

It is clear that Lewis's stress is upon the importance of imagination, even though his spokesman, the Professor, in speaking about Lucy's experience in *The Lion, the Witch, and the Wardrobe*, suggests that logic is to be respected, and is to be distinguished from "scientism." It is imagination which makes people more receptive to truth. Before they enter Narnia the children are thrilled at the environment in and around the Professor's house: they speculate about the rooms and corridors, the birds and animals, and they explore the woods. They are prepared for the Narnian experience by Romantic pre-experience, which prepares one for truths greater than our own imaginings. On the other hand, the threshold to the supernatural passes unrecognized by those who are imaginatively, and hence spiritually, closed. In *The Magician's Nephew* the witch Jadis doesn't realize the function and importance of the Wood between the Worlds, a sort of Black Hole by way of which one passes from one cosmos to another. Lewis writes: "I think her mind was of a sort which cannot remember that quiet place at all; however often you took her there and however long you left her there, she would still know nothing about it." Even the spiritually open may in stubbornness refuse to acknowledge God's presence and guidance. Peter confesses to Aslan in *Prince Caspian* that he had in fact realized the Lion was close to him even when he was in denial: "I really believed it was him tonight. . . . I mean, deep down inside. Or I could have, if I'd let myself. But I just wanted to get out of the woods—and—oh, I don't know." And some subjects, faced with spiritual reality, are unpersuadable, closed to actual experience. In the stable at the end of the world, in *The Last Battle*, the unbelieving dwarfs see only dark where others see and smell flowers. When Lucy offers them some violets, they feel insulted, for their impression is that she is "shoving a lot of filthy stable-litter in [their] face[s]." I leave the last word to Aslan: "They will not let us help them. They have chosen *cunning* instead of *belief*. Their prison is only in their own minds, yet they are in that prison; and so afraid of being taken in that they cannot be taken out. . . ."

C. S. LEWIS AND GOD'S SURPRISES

Charles Colson

OR . . . How the writings of a humble Oxford professor
helped to inspire a prison ministry that spans the globe

*Chuck Colson is a native of Boston who holds degrees from
Brown University and George Washington University. From
1969 to 1973 he served as Special Counsel to U.S. President
Richard Nixon. After spending nine months in a Federal prison
stemming from charges related to the Watergate affair, Colson
was released and in 1976 founded Prison Fellowship, an organization for ministering to prisoners, their families, and the victims of crime. Prison Fellowship, or "PF" as it is sometimes
abbreviated, now has chapters throughout the United States and
around the globe. Colson remains active in prison ministry, lob-
bying for legal reform through PF's Justice Fellowship branch,
and in his writing. Besides his regular columns for Prison
Fellowship's monthly newsletter, he also writes for* Christianity
Today *and has authored several books, including* Born Again,
Life Sentence, Kingdoms in Conflict, *and* Loving God. *This
piece first appeared in the June 1998 issue of* Jubilee Extra,
*copyright of Prison Fellowship Ministries, and is reprinted here
with permission.*

In 1998, I celebrated the twenty-fifth anniversary of my conversion to Christ. And what was it that turned around a hardened ex-marine, White House hatchet man? The loving witness of a friend and the writings of a tweedy, pipe-smoking scholar of medieval literature named C. S. Lewis. Because this year was also the celebration of the hundredth anniversary of Lewis's birth, I found myself reflecting on the manifold ways his writings had shaped my life and ministry.

It all began for me one evening in the home of Tom Phillips, a business colleague. Tom read a passage on pride from Lewis's *Mere Christianity*. Though I didn't let on, it was as if Lewis had written the words just for me. They pierced my heart, exposing my sin. That night, sitting in my car in Tom's driveway, I broke down in a flood of tears.

But I distrust emotional responses, and it was only by reading the entire book a week later that my intellect caught up with my spiritual experience. In a single page, Lewis demolished my complacent rationalization of Christ's demands, the notion that Jesus was merely a great moral teacher. Given the claims Jesus made to divinity, a moral teacher is precisely what he could not be, Lewis argued: Either he was indeed the Son of God or he was a scoundrel and a liar. Faced with this clear choice, I realized that the presence I confronted that night in the driveway was truly the living God.

But Lewis's influence did not stop there. His writings came to have a decisive influence on my entire ministry. Prison Fellowship's approach is indebted to Lewis's essay "The Humanitarian Theory of Punishment," which skewers the modern theory of criminal justice defining punishment in terms of deterrence or rehabilitation.[1] Such an approach is thoroughly pragmatic, Lewis points out: It presumes that criminal justice is about achieving sociological goals. And in the process it reduces the criminal to an object to be manipulated to reach those goals. Given such a dehumanizing view of the person, no wonder the theory invariably fails.

By contrast, a biblical understanding is thoroughly moral: Punishment is about justice. The criminal is accorded the dignity of being a moral agent, whose actions *deserve* either praise or punishment. This is the moral perspective undergirding Prison Fellowship's ministry.

Elsewhere, in my speaking and writing, I continue to be shaped by Lewis's writings. His *Miracles* (1947) was uncannily prophetic in foreseeing the emerging naturalistic philosophy, which has stripped the transcendent dimension from every area of thought, whether science or law or ethics—a theme I raise often in my speeches and radio commentaries. His *The Abolition of Man* (1943) dissected the moral relativism that has devastated modern education, from the college campus to the elementary classroom. In a chapter titled "Men Without Chests," Lewis puts his finger on the fatal flaw in all secular ethical systems: They address how to know what's right, but they cannot shape the will to *do* what's right. Finally, Lewis's eloquent arguments in *Mere Christianity* on why Christians must stand together to defend the faith have motivated my work to bring evangelicals and Catholics together.

It strikes me as a delicious irony that this quiet Oxford and Cambridge don should exert such a formative influence on me and many others today. He was a humble man, who probably never imagined his work would have such an impact. I picture him in his study, faded volumes of medieval literature stacked high on the shelves, thoughtfully puffing on his pipe (which is now one of my prized possessions, given to me by the executor of Lewis's estate).

Never would he have dreamed that his writings would inspire a prison ministry that spans the globe, along with a speaking and radio ministry reaching much of the church.

There is a lesson here for you and me, as each of us shoulders the task God has given us. Lewis exhorted Christians to get ready for the Second Coming simply by staying at our post, faithfully doing whatever we are called to do. And when we do, God will often use our efforts in ways we cannot imagine.

The God of whom C. S. Lewis wrote so movingly is still sovereign, and still surprises us with the way he works through humble human instruments—if only we are faithful.

THE PILGRIM'S REGRESS

J. I. Packer

When Kathryn Lindskoog's Finding the Landlord: A Guidebook to C. S. Lewis's Pilgrim's Regress *(Cornerstone Press) came out in 1995, J. I. Packer gave the following comments about his favorite Lewis book.*

Lewis wrote *The Pilgrim's Regress: An Allegorical Apology for Christianity, Reason and Romanticism* in 1932, within a year of his return to full Christian faith. He had been anchored in Oxford for fourteen years, for half that time teaching English at Magdalen College, and Oxford, intellectually speaking, was his whole world. As an adult don he was, as one would expect, a strong-minded, self-critical thinker; also, he was an unusually pugnacious debater, and a fairly sophisticated metaphysician of the pre-Moore-Ayer-Wittgenstein era. He wanted to be a poet, and had for years been researching allegory as a literary form in medieval poetry, preparing to write his masterpiece of 1936, *The Allegory of Love.* As a human being, however, it was his Celtic imagination and his boyish emotional makeup that gave shape to his identity. When, therefore, he wanted to tell the world about his twenty-year pilgrimage from reactionary atheism back to traditional orthodoxy, what flowed out of him—suddenly, during two hectic weeks—was an allegory, partly autobiographical, partly satirical, partly expository, which combined his childlike love of childlike narrative with his deep literary appreciation of *Pilgrim's Progress* as a successful allegory and a Christian classic, and his donnish devotion to didactic argument—in addition, of course, to allowing him to try out a few Christian poems. This was *The Pilgrim's Regress*, written as a work of art for an in-group of Christian highbrows in and around Oxford University, long before he ever dreamed he might become a popular author. (He actually subtitled it . . . *or Pseudo-Bunyan's Periplus* [a Greek word meaning 'circular voyage']—which shows how little he saw himself as writing for the general Christian public. We should be glad his first publisher cut that bit out.)

For *Regress's* third edition, from its third publisher (Geoffrey Bles, who was doing well with *The Problem of Pain* and *The Screwtape Letters*, and who clearly thought he could sell *Regress* too if Lewis could lighten it up), Lewis wrote a preface and added explanatory headlines on each page. In this 1943 preface he declared the book obscure and accounted for the obscurity by noting, first, that the personal pilgrimage it embodies was idiosyncratic, second that its philosophical milieu was passé, and third that labelling the lure of "Sweet Desire" (afterwards called *joy*) as "romanticism" was misleading. He also trashed the book's satire as bitter and uncharitable. I hear him, but I still find the flow clear, the childlikeness charming, and the satire scintillating and satisfying. The reason *Regress* floors so many of its readers is, I think, none of the above; it is, simply, that the book is so very *Oxford*, blending whimsy and wit with maturity, sophistication, and adolescence in a way that may well baffle strangers to this rather precious ethos. Only this, to my mind, can explain why Peter Kreeft and Chad Walsh, top Lewisians by any standard, find it "wooden" and "small-minded," and "mediocre" and "heavy," respectively, whereas I, reading it at Oxford in 1945 and again in Vancouver for this review, with several more readings in between, have always been entranced by it, experiencing it as head-clearing and at the same time heart-grabbing in a very special way. So, too, Lewis's Oxonian biographer George Sayer calls it "captivating" and says: "No other book of his is written with such a light touch, and few are so often witty and profound." Despite Lewis himself, I rate *Regress* truly quality work, as fine as anything else he ever produced.

And it need never floor anyone again; for Lindskoog's guidebook, written at undergraduate level out of actual teaching experience, explores its background, fills in its allusions, and points up its flow, in a clear and efficient way. It could fairly have been titled *All You Ever Wanted to Know About* The Pilgrim's Regress *But Were Afraid to Ask!* It cannot, to be sure, convey the haunting mythical flavour of the allegory itself, any more than a cookery book can tell us how a dish will taste to us when it is served; but it makes tuning in to *Regress* easier than it was before, and that is a real boon. Kathryn Lindskoog has given us a very useful book, which I heartily recommend.

FORTY YEARS' PERSPECTIVE

Bede Griffiths

Dom Bede Griffiths was an early Lewis pupil whose memoir of Lewis appears in C. S. Lewis at the Breakfast Table. *Griffiths served as a Benedictine monk in India for decades, authored several books, and was conversant in both Syriac and Sanskrit. The following piece was submitted to* The Canadian C. S. Lewis Journal *in response to comments from some of its constituents. First, Griffiths discusses "the personal heresy" that Lewis so disliked, the idea that studying an author's (or poet's) private life is in any way relevant to the meaning of the work they produced. (Muriel Jones, whose undergraduate papers Lewis marked, had mentioned that Lewis would not have liked all the attention given him by publications like* The Canadian C. S. Lewis Journal.*) Second, many former Lewis pupils have commented on the bullying and impersonal style Lewis used in his tutorials, while many others have recalled the tutorial sessions with fondness. Both impressions are believable. Lewis liked rational opposition and thought it a valuable part of his own tutorials under William T. Kirkpatrick ("The Great Knock") during his student days. ("Here was a man who thought not about you but about what you said," he wrote in* Surprised by Joy. *"Some boys would not have liked it; to me it was red beef and strong beer . . . . No doubt I snorted and* *bridled a little at some of my tossings; but, taking it all in all, I loved the treatment.") Surely this influenced Lewis's teaching method of dialectical criticism, hence the "bullying" and "impersonal" approach. On the other hand, Lewis seemed to be a little less "bullying" with female pupils, those who were shy yet industrious, and seemingly a little warmer to students who shared mutual admiration for some of Lewis's favorite authors (such as G. K. Chesterton or George MacDonald). Part of Griffiths' article is a response to Norman Bradshaw, a former pupil who found Lewis impersonal and intimidating. Third, there have been some people who feel that Lewis had a rather "dark" and sinister imagination, that the portraits he paints of evil people in his books— especially in his space trilogy—were themselves discomforting and wicked. Griffiths mentions one person of that persuasion—W. R. Fryer, also a former Lewis pupil—in discussing his views on the subject.*

As one who was a pupil of C. S. Lewis for two years and a fairly close friend for nearly forty years, perhaps I may be allowed to comment on a few questions raised about his tutoring style and his imagination.

In the first place I would entirely agree with Muriel Jones when she says that Lewis would have regarded all discussion about him as a person as irrelevant and would have been horrified at the very idea of a C. S. Lewis Society. I myself do not entirely share this view. I remember well how at one of my first tutorials when I spoke with approval of the sonnets of Sir Philip Sidney because he wrote from personal experience, he was most indignant and walked up and down in great agitation, maintaining that a poet's feelings had nothing to do with the value of his poetry. He developed this thesis in his controversy with Dr. Tillyard in their book *The Personal Heresy.* I don't agree with this, but there is no doubt that he felt very strongly about it and I am sure that his reaction to all this fuss about him as a person would have met with his stern disapproval. But that doesn't necessarily mean that he would have been right.

This brings me to the more general question of the behavior of Lewis in his tutorials. I must say that my experience was the exact opposite of that of Norman Bradshaw. I never found him in the least degree "aloof" in his attitude. On the contrary our tutorials would sometimes go on for hours after we had finished the real business and we would discuss everything under the sun. This was in fact the beginning of a lasting friendship and we continued in the same spirit for the rest of his life. Of course, he may have been different with other people, but that may have been their fault, not his.

I would also question the whole idea of his "dark imagination." To speak of him as being "obsessed with devils and hell" seems to me to be the exact opposite of the truth. He was naturally, as he always maintained, a "pagan," who enjoyed the natural world and the pleasures of the natural man. It was his reading of the New Testament which convinced him of the reality of sin and evil and compelled him to accept the doctrine of hell. I confess that I am not convinced by Professor Fryer's quotation from Westcott.[1] However much we may learn about the fire of God's love and the completeness of perfect justice, nothing can alter the fact that Jesus himself and the New Testament as a whole never questioned the possibility of final loss. In my opinion it is only possible to get beyond this if one is prepared to question the biblical tradition as a whole. In this respect I feel that Lewis was limited by his very biblical Christianity and what Muriel Jones calls his attachment to a "conservative, individualist Protestant tradition."

On the other hand, I think that it is unfair to attack Lewis's notion of God as one who "hems us in" and "corners us," because this was exactly Lewis's own experience, as he has described it in *Surprised by Joy*. Whether we like it or not, this is how God is experienced by many people, as the Book of Job makes only too clear. But once again this does not mean that Lewis had a negative view of God. He was immensely aware of the sheer love and grace which conversion had revealed to him and I would say that his under-standing of the nature of God was extremely balanced. He never lost sight of the "terrible" aspect of God (which everyone has to face) but he was no less firmly convinced of the infinity of love and grace.

To my mind the Narnia stories reveal Lewis's personal religion more profoundly than any of his more theological works. He wrote those other works more from his head, but the Narnia stories came from his heart. He just allowed himself to express his inmost feelings with complete spontaneity. The figure of Aslan in the Narnia stories tells us more of how Lewis understood the nature of God than anything else he wrote. It has all the hidden power and majesty and awesomeness which Lewis associated with God, but also all the glory and the tenderness and even the humor which he believed belonged to him, so that children could run up to him and throw their arms round him and kiss him. There is nothing of "dark imagination" or fear of devils and hell in this. It is "mere Christianity."

Holy Trinity Church, Headington Quarry, where the Lewis brothers attended weekly services.

I SLEEP BUT MY HEART WATCHETH

Martin Moynihan

Martin Moynihan studied at Oxford from 1934–1938 and was a pupil of C. S. Lewis while reading English during his final year there. He is the author of The Latin Letters of C. S. Lewis *and the translator of* Letters: C. S. Lewis, Don Giovanni Calabria: A Study in Friendship. *Mr. Moynihan served in the British diplomatic corps until his retirement. He now lives in Wimbledon Common.*

It's a cold wintry morning—still dark—and, snatching at your half-length gown, you are hastening—because the minute bell is tolling—you are hastening down the kitchen staircase and along the cloisters to eight o'clock morning Chapel. You are alone. But then, coming from the New Building along the cloisters past the library staircase, you hear a measured tread. Clomp, clomp, clomp. It is the gowned figure of C. S. Lewis.

Independently, you both pass into the engulfing glooms of the Chapel, he to his high-up Fellows' stall (left of the altar, as you face it), you (as directed by Tallboys the verger) to one of the stalls below. P. V. M. Beneke will also be there, along with Lewis, and from time to time, a sprinkling of irregulars—G. R. Driver, S. G. Lee, the President himself at times, George Gordon, and others too.

Adam Fox, the Chaplain and Dean of Divinity conducts the unvaried service of Morning Prayer, as found in the Book of Common Prayer: prayers, invitatory, responses, collects, lessons, the psalm for the day—with one of the lessons, perhaps, read from the lection by a Demy—say Charles Issawi, from Egypt, later of Princeton. In twenty minutes it is over and you all file out, dons first, into the day-to-be.

For my first years at Oxford that was all I knew of Lewis—and yet, looking back, how much that all was.

During those years I read Modern Greats under Harry Weldon. This was also to give me common ground with Lewis. At the end of my third term, i.e., prior to the Long Vac, Harry said to me, "Well, your philosophy papers are all right: but it is time you had a philosophy of your own." A philosophy of my own?! Then the penny dropped. Not enough to recount what others thought, however well described. Say what *you* think—do you agree with them or, if not, what do you yourself hold? Cycling home through the Welsh Marches, I puzzled over the Ontological argument, and reached the conclusion that it was sound (or that, if it did not prove God, it disproved any disproof). And so, on from there, to objective idealism—and Finals.

In the process, the Chapel acquired new meaning. "The last enchantments of the Middle Ages"? Those indeed. Abelard's Paris, Duns Scotus's Oxford—yes, but much more: the age-old theme, the ongoing debate: affirmation versus negation going back to Greece and on to what was going on all around you in Oxford and still is: the perennial philosophy against its whatever current alternatives. The names change, the debate continues.[1] Lewis was part of this debate and Chapel aligned him with the way of affirmation. When, in my fourth year, I came to read English with him (and Anglo-Saxon with C. L. Wrenn) this alignment was something we both knew and it needed no saying. Not that it stopped there or meant general approval. "Your essay on Wordsworth, good. But: pan-Kantian of course." Poetry, remember, is more than philosophy.

And so, from recalling the cloisters, I have passed to the New Buildings. Up those broad wooden stairs (with windows overlooking the Deer Park), up to the lofty white panelled room—"Come in!"—with Lewis deep in one huge cloth-covered armchair and the other huge chair, opposite, for yourself. Anything less like *Shadowlands* could hardly be imagined. In the film, three or four young men sit, bolt upright on a row of high-backed stools while Lewis booms down at them without a pause. In reality you had an hour with Lewis alone, read him an essay, received his comments and then shared the ever-widening conversation which ensued. It was intellectual friendship, to the limit of your ability. He was generous and forbearing. Like Johnson, he liked to go for a kill but was equally quick with *touché*. He liked the rigor of the game. He could rebuke. "In your essay you have used a quotation quoted by Bradley—but without attribution. I regard that as a gross blemish." He was never little. The S. C. R. discussed what painter would best paint each of the Fellows. To Lewis, they unanimously allotted Rubens.

After a while, I was invited to join his Thursday evening Beowulf parties—Beer and Beowulf as they came to be known. All I now remember of Anglo-Saxon is not Beowulf but the Battle of Maldon:

> Hige sceal the heardra, heorte the cenre,
> Mod sceal the maere, the ure maegen lytlath.

> Will shall be the firmer, hearts the keener,
> Courage the greater, as our strength lessens.

In 1938, the war clouds gathering over Europe (to quote Auden, "though sombre the sixteen skies of Europe and the Danube flood"). What fitting lines, to lead one on to the Battle of Britain. As it was, week by week, you would take it in turns to read some lines of Beowulf aloud and discussion would follow. This quickly ranged afar. "Do you believe," asked someone who did believe in it, "do you believe in the Divine Right of Kings?" "To put it in context, you have to go back," said Lewis carefully, "to St. Paul's Epistle, where it says that the powers that be are ordained by God."[2] "O, but I don't believe in God." General laughter. "You believe in the divine but not in God?" "Well, what is God?" That's a facer, one thought. "God," said Lewis, "is self-subsistent being, cause of himself." Aquinas, Hooker—how characteristic! The late Dom Bede Griffiths quoted Lewis as saying in a letter "but surely you would believe that God is a concrete individual?" Coleridge said if he found a line by Wordsworth alone in a desert, he would at once recognize the authorship and exclaim, "Wordsworth!" So here. "Lewis!" And, when you think that Dom Bede wrote years and years after Lewis's death, you see how history, recorded long after, can be as true as history written at the time.

What a joy it was to be asked by Barbara Reynolds to translate into English the Latin letters which she had discovered in photostat in Wheaton: a correspondence passing between Don Giovanni Calabria and C. S. Lewis 1947–1954.[3] They were, as I wrote at the time, limpid and deeply refreshing. And they combined dogmatics and daily living in a wonderful way. (In the translation Monica Moynihan helped; and I was greatly indebted to Colin Hardie, himself an Inkling, who most kindly acted as long-stop, to prevent howlers of mine from reaching print.)

Thinking of the *Letters*, I am reminded of the sympathetic view which Lewis took, *qua* poetry, of Dryden's Hind and the Panther and of the passage where the Hind (representing Catholicism) looks up, saying to the truth-seeker, "she, whom ye seek, am I." Little wonder Don Giovanni admired Lewis for his evenly balanced view of Northern Ireland. Of each extreme Lewis wrote that they "know not of what Spirit they are." "*Te beatum dico*," replied Don Giovanni, "*te beatum dico et dicam*."[4]

After going down I kept in touch from time to time but then, to spare Lewis, I ceased writing. With Monica, I last met him in Cambridge after hearing his Cambridge inaugural which, looking back, seems even more prophetic than it did at the time. "On the Naming of Times." How they change. No one, more than the author of *The Allegory of Love* knew and said this. Courtly love gave place to family love (Spenser) and then came also romantic love; and that, too, might pass. In his St. John Fisher lecture, Cardinal Ratzinger joined with Lewis in identifying *moralis relativismus* (see *The Latin Letters*), moral relativity, as the sign and weakness of our epoch.

The last time I heard by letter from Lewis was in the Far East, on the eve of our re-invasion of Burma. He quoted, in Greek, from the Greek Anthology, Plato's lines on the Euboeans, fallen in Persia, and "how far they lie from their native land." He hoped the lines would not apply to me; and, thankfully, they did not.

In Oxford I once called on Lewis (unannounced) after a drive through Burford. I had been into the churchyard there and had identified the tomb—an altar tomb near the church—of Meade Faulkner, of Armstrong Whitworths, uncle of a friend, and *inter alia*, author of *Moonfleet* and the *Nebuly Coat* (see the tablet in Durham Cathedral). Round the tomb (I told Lewis) was a Latin inscription; and I wondered what it was. As I quoted, I could see Lewis going into bottom gear.

"*Ego dormio!*" I am sleeping. "*Sed cor meum vigilat*"? But my heart is awake—my heart . . . it is the Shulamite! It is from the Song of Songs! "I sleep but my heart watcheth."[5]

For me, to recall Lewis is to recall Magdalen, those large rooms in the New Building, on sunny days or winter evenings, with the Cher and the Deer Park near by and the lawn leading to the Cloisters. And when I think of Lewis's grave in Trinity churchyard in Headington, I apply to him those lines which he so seized upon from the Song of Songs:

Ego dormio sed cor meum vigilat.

INTELLECTUAL DEVELOPMENT

Joan O'Hare

Joan O'Hare was a wartime pupil of Lewis's while studying at St. Hilda's College, Oxford, in the early 1940s. She lives in England, making her home in Blackburn, Lancashire.

Almost fifty years after the event one cannot vouch for the accuracy of one's memory. I was basically a nonacademic person and my career has lain in work with people, and not with literature. I was very conscious of this trait when dealing with Oxford academics and always nervous of them. Also I was the product of a local high school who acquired an education by having a quick brain and innate ability to concentrate deeply, which led to the winning of scholarships—my schooling and college days were provided by the State. I was definitely working class in origin, had a North Country accent and a total naiveté of polite social forms. Thus it was not easy to be an undergraduate at Oxford in 1939.

At the end of Hilary term 1941, together with another student at St. Hilda's College, I was called in by my tutor. Quietly and impressively we were told that in Trinity term we were to go for joint tutorials to C. S. Lewis. As he had not hitherto accepted women students, this was a great honor, and we were to be on our best behavior, work hard, and ensure that we were not also the last women students he accepted. A preliminary appointment had been made.

This foreword was not calculated to give confidence, and matters were compounded by my fellow student who made me feel very nervous. We were complete opposites. She was very feminine, attractive, suave, and sophisticated with a very BBC voice and, above all, the dignity of a flowing scholar's gown. We set off together, my colleague in trailing red floral creation, myself in dark brown tailored costume and brown tie on an old white school blouse. My skimpy undergraduate gown was the gift of an Oxonian schoolmistress when I left school. It came with a ragged hole in the back, the result of a burn. (The short gown could be used in place of a newspaper to improve the draught when lighting a coal fire in one's room.) When it came to making an impression, we two obviously were at variance. To me, C. S. Lewis was a name greatly venerated by a respected schoolteacher as the author of *The Allegory of Love*, which I had found extremely difficult. My inferiority complex was rampant by the time we reached New Building in Magdalen College.

A large, well-built tweedy man rose to greet us—at least he seemed large to me, and I thought he looked more like an angler than a don. The meeting was urbane and businesslike. We would study Milton. We would each prepare a weekly assignment. One of us would write an essay on the assignment and read it aloud in tutorial. The other would then discuss the points made and criticize. Writing and criticism would alternate. It seemed fair, if one had not already been overawed by having to share tutorials with a scholar. On the way back to college, my colleague proposed a pact—we would be sparing of our criticism and treat each other's essay gently. My spirits rose—I had survived a first encounter with the great man, and my fellow was perhaps not as inhuman as I thought she was. It did not occur to me to wonder what were the feelings of a tutor when confronted with two utterly disparate students. Whatever his feelings of dismay or doubt, they were concealed by impeccable courtesy.

On going down from Oxford, I kept very little connected with academic work, and if any written records of the tutorials or any essays had been around, they would have been destroyed then. The chief import of the tutorials and the intellectual impact were absorbed as part of one's internal development and are lost to conscious memory. At the conscious level, only trivialities remain.

Milton was a long-established favorite with me, especially the verse-dramas and *Paradise Lost*. I must have coasted through tutorials on work I had done in school. It fell to me, however, to prepare the essay on Milton's prose works, with which I was unfamiliar. I scrambled an essay together at the last minute, read it, and sat back unworried, waiting for my fellow-student's remarks. In view of our mutual pact of noncriticism, I was overwhelmed when she came out with a blistering attack on everything I had said, ending by saying that I was talking rubbish in saying that Milton argued—he never argued. Weakly I said that I had not written that Milton argued, I wrote that "Milton wrote argumentatively to persuade." "I cannot defend myself beyond that," I concluded. "Can't you?" thundered the master, "I can." And he did. How he demolished the attack on me I do not remember, but his kindness and support I have never forgotten.

The only other memory is of the day when my fellow student had not done her essay. She asked me to present her apologies and say she was unwell. This was, after all, the summer term, and the tennis courts were in the garden and the river and boat house at the end of the garden. So, as the student not required to present the essay, my own preparation had been less than meticulous, and my only desire was to escape the threat of a full hour closeted one-to-one with one of the most formidable intellects in Oxford after grossly inadequate preparation. Self-discipline alone took me to the tutorial, where no doubt I blushed and stammered about "not serious" and "headache, I think," convinced that C. S. Lewis knew exactly what was going on. Certainly we started with a cursory look at the week's assignment, but somehow we drifted from that to general conversation. He tried me on astronomy but kindly did not pursue a subject of which I was totally ignorant. He made a semiplayful attack on undergraduates who wasted time in coffee shops (Fuller's and the Cadena) instead of attending lectures. I dared not say they were exercising their critical powers very often, in attending good and skipping bad lectures, so I tried to defend them by saying time was not always wasted and some intelligent conversation took place; when it came to coffee drinking, I quoted Gibbon about the dull and deep potations of the seniors excusing the brisk intemperance of youth. It does not now seem apposite but it drew the response "Ah! I am a secret cocoa drinker." There was no explanation and the conversation drifted away to some other topic. At the end of the statutory hour we parted. I was surprised that he had labored so long with such unpromising material, but I assumed that this was real conscientiousness—an hour was promised, an hour was given. Looking back one regrets the lost opportunity but at the time I was concerned only with trying not to look a fool. I suspect he was preventing me by adapting his level to mine.

Later, when *The Screwtape Letters* were published, it seemed to me a full expression of the man I had met in that tutorial and again I relished the balanced argument, sly humor and skilful prose.

Incidentally when my end of term report arrived from him it was not only kind and tolerant of my studies—it was perceptive of my personality to a greater degree than any other report on me in my three years at Oxford. My college principal was surprised and thought she knew me better than he did, but I knew that he was right. He was not only a great intellect, he was a great human being, and if I brought little of academic interest from him, I gained personally from his kindness and tolerance.

Since typing the above I have realized that the influence of CSL was greater than I thought. For instance *The Screwtape Letters* had considerable impact now I analyze it. For me they shed light on human personality and their humor enabled me to be more relaxed and tolerant of human frailties. As my working life has been in social work, this improvement in understanding and attitude has been far more important to me than anything I gained academically. And the knowledge was acquired painlessly—indeed with enjoyment.

Pulpit, Mansfield College Chapel. Here Lewis preached his famous Pentecost Sunday sermon, "Transposition." (Photo by Peter Cousin)

COURTESY AND LEARNING

Pat Wallsgrove

Pat Wallsgrove was a student of St. Hilda's College, Oxford, who studied with Lewis during the Second World War. After graduating, she went on to teach English for many years at various institutions and watched her four children grow up. She is now enjoying her retirement in the pleasant midland English town of Leamington Spa.

I was indeed tutored by C. S. Lewis, and was interested to read the reminiscences of Mrs. Cowan and Mrs. Berry.[1] I endorse their impressions though I did not think him ugly—more like a jovial farmer than the sensitive scholar and supreme wordsmith that he was. I was sent to Mr. Lewis with Helen Tyrrell, in my final year at St. Hilda's, by Helen Gardner, my literary and personal tutor. Ostensibly the subject was study for the B.11 paper of the Final Examinations, which covered general literary history and concepts. I am not sure why we were the only ones Miss Gardner chose, because we were not her cleverest pupils. Perhaps it was because we both had interests and activities in Oxford outside the course of study—Helen's were religious and philosophical, mine were sporting and political. Perhaps (and this occurred to me much later, and Helen Gardner is alas! no longer here to refute it) it was because we were tolerably good looking, and as we were I think the first pupils she sent to Mr. Lewis, Miss Gardner was not above wishing to make a good impression on him.

We presented ourselves weekly at Mr. Lewis's rooms in the charming eighteenth-century block of Magdalen College known as the New Buildings. Mr. Lewis, in his carpet slippers and surrounded by piles of books and papers, always treated us with courtesy and listened to our essays with charity, and encouraged us to talk. I remember little of the subjects discussed, though the man is a vivid memory.

On one occasion he greeted us with a description of the curious letters he received—that morning it was a long discourse on the mystical significance of the Egyptian pyramids—he was of course well known by then as a broadcaster and writer, and received a large correspondence. I remember *The Screwtape Letters* as obligatory reading among my contemporaries when it was published. We were also aware that he and Professor Tolkien were friends and were both producing works of imagination. My own children were brought up on the *Narnia* books, and I recall my twelve-year-old grandson requesting a complete set as his present for Christmas in 1987.

I encountered Mr. Lewis in my first year in Oxford by attending (with as many other undergraduates of all schools as could cram into the medieval hall at Magdalen) his lectures on "Prolegomena to Sixteenth-Century Studies." I have my notes on these lectures and some—incomplete I think—on the following year's "Prolegomena to Renaissance Studies." The former were of great use to me, together with his *Preface to Paradise Lost*, when I was introducing students to Milton.

May I recommend to your readers the dramatization of C. S. Lewis's latter life made by the BBC, in which Joss Ackland portrayed him—most faithfully according to my memory. But then Joss Ackland also knew Oxford in the 1940s, as his sister was a contemporary of mine at St. Hilda's. Like Mrs. Cowan and Mrs. Berry, I will always be grateful for the chance of knowing C. S. Lewis, and delighted that interest in him and his writings is being maintained.

WARTIME TUTOR

Helen Tyrrell Wheeler

Mrs. Helen Tyrrell Wheeler was another wartime pupil of C. S.
Lewis whom Pat Wallsgrove mentions in the previous chapter.
She writes "From 1941 to 1945 I was at St. Hilda's College,
Oxford: C. S. Lewis acted as my tutor for two separate terms.
From Oxford I went to Christ's Hospital, Horsham (the famous
Bluecoat school) for four years, before taking up a post, with my
mathematician husband, at the English School, Cairo (Egypt). In
1951 we settled in Tonbridge in Kent. Here my time was shared
between three children and a very happy experience of adult
education. I gave classes for the departments of external educa-
tion run by Oxford and by the University of Kent, published two
small books and acted as a tutor—counselor for the Open
University since its foundation."

What do I remember of my tutorials with Lewis? I vividly
remember walking through Magdalen grounds to go to tutorials: it
was high summer and I could see the deer in the distance. The
whole seems to have merged with landscapes in *Aristo* and *The
Fairy Queen,* and I always think of them in such visual terms, pre-
sumably because of CSL. His study, too, is clear. My other tutors,
Dame Helen Gardner and Lord David Cecil, lived in elegant,

orderly eighteenth-century rooms which always seemed full of brightness: sunshine or firelight or both. Quite different was Lewis's. There were of course books everywhere, but that was true of every room one went into in Oxford. These books had *taken over*—so that comfort had long departed. It was quite a business to find seats for the three of us there because women students usually went in pairs to men tutors. And the room was curiously shadowy, with what I think were heavy dark curtains over other mysterious doors. It was, after all, wartime, with little fuel and pervasive draughts. Through these obscure entries there would, now and again, appear a very stealthy figure, who with a murmured greeting would track down a wanted book and disappear again into limbo. This, we gathered, was Lewis's brother. Informed opinion in Oxford at the time held that he was the world's greatest authority on all those families of that French aristocracy who had suffered during the Revolution; and that he knew the tiniest detail of their disastrous lives. I have no idea if this interesting belief is correct.[1]

I think I went to CSL for two separate terms, one of which was devoted to Spenser and Milton; and I am pretty sure we managed to include Malory, Tasso, and Sir Walter Scott. I had always loved Scott and had been chagrined upon growing up to find him in critical disfavor: so it was particularly reassuring to encounter CSL's measured and loving appreciation of him. Of all the texts at this time, the one round which most lively debate fizzed was *Paradise Lost*. The *Preface* came out in 1942, and arguments about the moral position of Satan were to be heard in the Kardomah, the Shamrock, on punts, and everywhere that single-minded English Literature students congregated. A small share of this enthusiasm may have been in reaction to the apparently dismal failure of some Cambridge pundits to appreciate the greatness of Milton. Much more, however, was owed to a special tang in the air of Oxford at that time and which was specially linked with the figures of CSL and his entirely enchanting friend, Charles Williams, poet, novelist and critic who had moved to Oxford at the beginning of the war.

It is typical that both men wrote books—startling in subject at that time—which brought heaven, hell, damnation, and the devil into a convincingly drab and ordinary thirties and forties context. Williams's "supernatural thrillers" such as *Descent into Hell* (1937) were popular enough to be on most library shelves. In 1940 CSL recast the idea in a considerably more acrid and contentious style with *The Screwtape Letters*. The devil ceased to be a reassuringly distant figure confined to mediaeval and Renaissance texts and instead had all the sharp know-how of the slipperiest salesman of a very large organization indeed, as successful as it was sinister. The movement of ideas swept forwards to produce the slick, city devil: equally it moved backwards to reaffirm the actuality of that moral and spiritual life which had inspired and pervaded all great literary works: this it was, both Lewis and Williams argued, that had *made* them great. Was it Williams who revived the Coleridgean word *coinherence?* Certainly it seemed to be the banner word of the time, and it was to have revealed the *coinherence* of the most disparate texts, times, dilemmas, and ideas that people crowded out the lectures of both Williams and Lewis. The former would give single lectures on subjects like marriage and divorce; the latter's most memorable series was a vast panoramic survey of the intellectual-rhetorical-literary influences which fed into the Renaissance.

One of the innumerable clubs that flourished briefly at this time was the Socratic Club of which I was for a few terms the secretary. We had a modest subscription, a healthy membership, a neat little yellow card listing the topics for our Monday discussions and above all, C. S. Lewis as our president. It was of course only by his prestige that the Club was able to attract its speakers or its membership; but for a time it was popular and lively with distinguished theologians ready to shepherd questioners into the paths of truth. Professor Quick, Father Martin D'Arcy, S.J., and of course Charles Williams came: the last to bring Dante's poetry into that kind of vivid and relevant life that most of that parochial little group of students could otherwise not have envisaged. I have a strong visual memory of these evenings, always associated with lamplight inside and total blackout without, of a big sprawling comfortable room with as many people sitting on the floor as in the old-fashioned immense armchairs and C. S. Lewis hurrying over Magdalen Bridge from his rooms to preside. He always established an immense, though rather impersonal, geniality and with his bright eyes and ruddy farmer's cheeks looked not unlike a mediaeval illustration of a fiery seraphim, though dressed in decent academic black. Sometimes he could not come, and the debate after the initial paper would miss his substantial confidence, his ability to rejig doubts into apparently axiomatic truths. He would have made an excellent barrister, or the kind of mediaeval theologian who always triumphed in the great academic debates.

My last memory of him is in 1945. Charles Williams had died suddenly—a huge congregation attended the funeral service at St. Cross Church and then spilled out among the green mounds of the churchyard. It had been, in typical Charles Williams' style, a very joyous, triumphant sort of service and I had an unforgettable final vision of CSL nimbly hovering between the sunlit gravestones very like a figure from the great Stanley Spencer picture of the resurrection in Cookham.

It was much later, when I had children of my own, that his *Narnia* books appeared, as did *The Lord of the Rings* by that other hero of the Oxford lecture halls, J. R. R. Tolkien. His lectures too, usually held in the Taylorian, were packed out largely because of the extraordinary pressure of excitement that swept over his audience when he broke (as he frequently did) into a Bardic rendering of *Beowulf*. Where else in the world would one be able to hear the hypnotic rhythms and crashing, criss-crossing alliterations of this poem delivered with such (we thought) impeccable authenticity of inflection? And if it was not impeccably authentic, then it ought to be, for the effect of spellbound attention was unfailing. It was very interesting to superimpose on my Oxford memory of these two formidable men, the subsequent images produced by their imaginations when freed from academic intentions. Each writer unmistakably continues in a different manifestation his own intrinsic self; the difference between these two great friends is absolute.

I was up at Oxford at a time when every material comfort was in short supply: food, clothes, and fuel were rationed. Travel within England was uncomfortable and slow, money for students was very short, fire-watching, or other war work, was part of every student's week, and the war and war news had become an abrasive condition of life. But at few times can there have been such splendidly exciting lectures and such overflowing lecture halls: *coinherence* was Charles Wiliams's label for the quality they believed in. What it meant to my generation of English Language and Literature undergraduates was that what happened in the great books was of equal significance to what happened in life, indeed that they were the same, and that to this importance, time could make no difference if you read the text as it should be read—"as one of those upon whom nothing can possibly be lost."

Magdalen College, New Building. Lewis's rooms are on the second floor.

A DEBT REPAID

Martin Lings

Martin Lings graduated with a B.A. from Oxford in 1932 and went on to lecture in the University of Kaunas (in Lithuania) on Anglo-Saxon and Middle English from 1935 to 1939. From 1940 to 1951 he held a lectureship in English Literature at Cairo University in Egypt where he lectured mainly on Shakespeare. In 1952 he returned to England and took a degree in Arabic from the University of London. He was the Assistant Keeper in the Department of Oriental Printed Books and Manuscripts of the British Museum from 1955 to 1970, the Deputy Keeper in 1970, and was made Keeper in 1971. Besides his many scholarly books, he has published The Elements and Other Poems *(1967), the preface to which contains some interesting facts about his friendship with his former Oxford tutor, C. S. Lewis.*

Lewis mentioned Lings and another undergraduate Adrian Hugh Paterson (who was later serving as lecturer at Cairo University when killed by an accident while riding in the Egyptian desert with Lings in July 1940) in a letter to his friend Arthur Greeves, "I wish you knew my two pupils, Lings and Paterson. Both are poets (quite promising I think) and fast friends of each other. They are just in the state you and I remember so well—the whole world of beauty opening upon them—and as

they share the same digs they must have a glorious time. One or other of them often accompanies me on my afternoon walk.
   "You can imagine how I enjoy them both. Indeed this is the best part of my job. In every given year the pupils I really like are in a minority; but there is hardly a year in which I do not make some real friend. I am glad to find that people become more and more one of the sources of pleasure as I grow older."

When I left school I had no real ambition beyond that of writing poetry. After two years at Oxford I had written a masque, which was performed at Magdalen College in 1930. At that time C. S. Lewis was English tutor at Magdalen. Whether he attended a performance I cannot remember, but I sent him a copy of the masque and he wrote back: "I have a very clear-cut idea of the difference between poetry and mere verse, and this is poetry beyond a doubt." But he evidently had reserves about it, as well he might, and some months later (by that time I had moved over from Classics to English, and he was my tutor) I handed him a short narrative poem and he wrote: "You have changed from being a young man who merely writes poetry to a young man who has written a poem—not a very great poem, but none the less a poem, a unity with a distinct flavor all its own which it keeps from beginning to end."

Later I was to incur other more considerable debts, and these have been acknowledged implicitly in my other writings. But the debt to Lewis has not yet been acknowledged and, for my own sake rather than for his, I am proud to boast of his appreciation. I take this opportunity of saying how much I owe to him, both for his encouragement, which went much further than I have said, and also, for his implacable criticism. Perhaps I owe even more, in both respects, to my friend Adrian Paterson, to whose memory *The Elements and Other Poems* is dedicated. He himself was a poet through and through, and left behind him, at his early death, some poems of rare beauty, none of which have yet been published.

He also was Lewis's pupil, at the same time as myself. It was our tutor's teaching of Old English poetry that made us realize, amongst other more important things, the deep affinity that still exists between our language and the ancient meter in which *Beowulf* is written. This alliterative meter, with its frequent clash of stressed syllables, I have used for all my later poems which are, as regards their form, the fruit of my apprenticeship to it in those early years. But above all it was from Lewis that we first learned the surpassing greatness of the Middle Ages, and it was he who fired us to snatch up, on the basis of Latin, enough Italian to read the *Divine Comedy* in the original, for he was of the opinion that there was nothing in English poetry that could approach Dante's epic.

Magdalen College Tower, Oxford. Like so many others, Lewis climbed the stairs to the roof for the annual May Day celebration (c.f. page 80).

AWE AND DELIGHT

Patricia M. Hunt

Mrs. Patricia M. Hunt, M.A. (nee Longuet-Higgins) lives in Turvey near Bedford, England. She was a student at Lady Margaret Hall 1940–43 and during part of that time had tutorials with Lewis.

An article in *The Canadian C. S. Lewis Journal* from one of Lewis's women students chimed in well with my own experience; but I was surprised to read that he treated her "like a princess" as my own impression was that he was very noncommittal and anxious not to step out of line in any way.[1] I went to him for tutorials in the Lent term of 1942, if I remember correctly, along with three other undergraduates of the English school at Lady Margaret Hall. We were to study a rather arid period of English literature, between Chaucer and the early Tudor writers such as Thomas More and Sir Philip Sydney. The period included such writers as Lydgate, Gower, Skelton, and so on—not very thrilling. Our English tutor had chosen to send us to Lewis for this period, and I doubt if anyone else could have made it more interesting. I had already made acquaintance with Lewis's writings, both literary and religious. Our English studies had required us to read his *Allegory of Love*, and *A Preface to Paradise Lost*, and my tutor had lent me his *The Problem of Pain,* which had recently come out. I think *Screwtape* appeared about this time too. My family members were also avid listeners to his *Broadcast Talks,* which were later printed. Apart from his books, which I found fascinating from the beginning, there were his lectures in Magdalen Hall on "Prolegomena to English Mediaeval Literature" and "Prolegomena to English Renaissance Literature," which were always crowded out. You have already a description of them. I will add that they were absolutely enthralling, both in their content, which was satisfyingly informative, and in the manner of their delivery, which was authoritative, humorous, and forthright.

As to the tutorials themselves, I think the fact that they were given to us by the great C. S. Lewis filled us with awe and delight. As far as I remember he was very quiet and not very talkative. I know we were spurred on to do our very best by his reputation, and get more out of this unpromising period than we would have thought possible. At one point I was set to write an essay on "The Ballad," and I know I made one of the best essays I wrote during my time at Oxford simply because I was writing it for C. S. Lewis. I had to read it aloud, and afterwards made copious notes on it of everything he said. It has now, alas, been jettisoned as a result of moving around the world; but I know I surprised myself by the number and variety of ideas I managed to produce on the Ballad! I can't remember much of what he said, if indeed he said an awful lot. It was mainly the effect he had on us which made these tutorials memorable. His study was shabby and comfortable, very masculine, with lots of books and papers around. Not much room for four women students to sit! (Or perhaps we were in pairs: I can't now remember.) He wore comfortable shabby clothes, a brown tweed jacket and grey flannel trousers, and smoked a pipe thoughtfully while we read aloud. He was always perfectly polite, but rather distant in manner, as if he was not used to women. His tutorials remain in my memory as one of the most stimulating experiences of my life.

Since those days, I have read every book by Lewis I have been able to get hold of; in fact, we own most of them, religious books, science fiction and Narnia Tales which my five children used to know almost by heart, and including his slim volumes of talks, sermons and essays. The latest have been his letters and poems, both borrowed from libraries and not owned. He has been one of the fundamental influences in my life, and I am very glad to be able to acknowledge this, and write this brief memoir in gratitude.

Radcliffe Camera, Bodleian Library, Oxford

University College; Lewis's college as a student

SPLENDID TUTOR

W. J. B. Owen

W. J. B. Owen was reading English as an undergraduate at Oxford when World War II broke out. He later went on to an English professorship at McMaster University in Hamilton, Ontario, Canada.

My acquaintance with C. S. Lewis was quite short: he was my tutor during my final year in the English School at Oxford, 1940–41; I entered the forces shortly afterwards, until 1946, inside and (mainly) outside Britain, so that chances to maintain contact were few. But I am glad to have had him for a teacher, for he was a splendid tutor, and I appreciated him in that role rather than as a lecturer. I found at least some of his lectures given to oversimplification, as if he were saying, "The problem is easy if you look at it this way"; but sometimes the problem was more difficult than he made it. But as a tutor he was superb: he would sit with notebook and pencil poised as he listened to my essay, and when it was finished he was ready with praise or criticism. The praise was brief, a few words only, but always gratifying. The criticism was searching but mildly presented: could that phrase not be recast? would that idea not be better if developed in such a way? and so forth. I learned much of scholarly method and clear thinking from this process, and also, perhaps, a gracious approach to pupils which I tried to adopt as a teacher myself.

In addition to weekly sessions in preparation for the final English School, I attended lectures which Lewis gave to B. Litt. candidates on textual criticism (the art of editing texts), which no doubt derived from his study of the classics. I found these especially useful in more recent times in preparing my editions of *Wordsworth's Prose* (Oxford, 1974; with J. W. Smyser) and *The Prelude* (Cornell, 1985). I regret that Lewis did not see these books; I think they would have pleased him.

When I came to Oxford in 1939, Lewis's reputation depended primarily on *The Allegory of Love*, generally recognized as a brilliant book. I heard the substance of his Bangor lectures in Oxford in 1939–40, and found his approach fresh and stimulating as a counter to the then more or less prevailing view of Milton as a covert Satanist. They were the best lectures I heard from him there.

I have read few of Lewis's writings outside of the field of English literature. I enjoyed the science-fiction trilogy, a good deal of it based on *Paradise Lost* and, therefore, recalling the lectures just mentioned. The more formally religious works I found not to my taste, and likewise I did not care for the Narnia series, though my children read them with pleasure. In this I seem to be in the minority, but it does not detract from my respect for him as a fine scholar or from my gratitude for his splendid teaching.

UNCROWNED
KING OF OXFORD

Rachel Trickett

Rachel Trickett was an undergraduate at Lady Margaret Hall from 1942–1945. She later returned to Oxford as English Tutor at St. Hugh's in 1954, becoming principal there in 1973, and served at that post until her retirement in 1991. This piece originally appeared in The Daily Telegraph, *November 13, 1983, and is reprinted here with permission.*

President Kennedy was assassinated on November 22, 1963. On the same day, two outstanding figures in the world of letters died— Aldous Huxley and C. S. Lewis.[1] "O, proud Death, What feast is toward in thine eternal cell?" seems the appropriate tag for the occasion. Of these and the many others invited on that date, none could lay a better claim than Lewis to be the most interesting guest. Not the most important; simply the most interesting.

When I was an undergraduate in Oxford between 1942 and 1945, Lewis was the uncrowned king not only of the English faculty but of the whole university. His influence was widespread through the Socratic Club, an undergraduate society for the dissemination of philosophical and theological ideas of which he was the most active senior member.

We made our way weekly through the blackout to hear this extraordinary man, whose formal lectures, "Prolegomena to Renaissance Studies," were less frequently attended, their learning being above our heads, their wit outside our range. We went to the Socratic Club to hear him in his element—the shrewd debater, the apologist, and popularizer, "the true warfaring Christian" in Milton's phrase.

His appearance, scarcely that of a crusader, looked like a high-living pugnacious butcher or grocer; his manner was bluff and no-nonsense. But his method of argument was Chestertonian, with all Chesterton's gaiety and nimble command of paradox. Even those who would have defied his ascendancy were disarmed on these occasions. His enjoyment of "the spite and mischief of the fray" was infectious. He had the Irishman's native delight in argument for its own sake; he loved to win and made no secret of it. And he won in such style that "e'en the ranks of Tuscany could scarce forbear to cheer."

But that was Lewis's public face. Pupils who survived the combat of his tutorials learned to love and rely on his humanity and loyalty and his stealthy generosity. None of the royalties he earned from his immensely popular theological books went into his own pocket. He had a simple way of following doctrines of perfection and gave anonymously, to widows, orphans, and any deserving case brought to his notice, the money he earned through public success.

By nature shy and reserved, he was, where feelings and beliefs were involved, devoted. Yet, except among pupils, disciples, and close friends, he was never popular with his peers. The old academic sin of envy destroyed Lewis's position in Oxford.

If ever a scholar-critic should have been honored in his own university by election to a chair, it was Lewis. But he ended his career as a professor at Cambridge. When in the fifties, a majority of the English faculty petitioned the electors to the Merton Chair to recall him from Cambridge, it was already too late. The prophet remained without honor in his own university.

But not without influence, which spreads out even now well beyond the confines of academe. The success of *The Screwtape Letters* and his other popular works of theology was the immediate occasion of the cry against him. Then, more than now, to be popular was to be less a scholar.

Inevitably younger medievalists rose up to refute the underlying assumption of the book that brought Lewis to fame—*The Allegory of Love*, one of the most original works of scholarship of the twentieth century. But which of his refuters ever persuaded a student actually to read Gower, or to take Spenser seriously, as Lewis had done? For this was his triumph. *The Preface to Paradise Lost*, perverse and paradoxical in many ways, forced us for the first time since the romantic critics adopted Satan as hero, to take Milton's theology as seriously as his poetry and to relate them.

In that great work, *English Literature in the Sixteenth Century*, all the old tricks of paradox and prejudice are plain. When Lewis boldly observes that he uses the words *drab* and *golden* of early and late Tudor poetry with no pejorative connotations in the former, his impudence takes our breath away. But the brilliant introductory chapter tumbles over with ideas that are a source of intellectual discovery.

Those colleagues who knew him well, and liked him, speak of his shyness, his modesty and his lack of self-knowledge. This last was the effect of a profound innocence. He believed that he represented the tastes and opinions of the ordinary man. In fact he was the most extraordinary of men. Everything in his life reflects this extraordinariness: his long submissive relationship with the widowed mother of a dead friend from the First World War; his central influence on the Inklings, a society which included such remarkable men as Charles Williams and J. R. R. Tolkien; his modesty with regard to them—he believed that they were each his superior and did nothing to promote his own children's stories and fiction which have since outpaced in popularity Williams's work, though not Tolkien's; his late experience of sexual love in marriage and his exceptional account of this in *The Four Loves* as well as his description of the effect of his wife's death in *A Grief Observed* are both aspects of the unusual nature of the man and his experience.

He possessed to an extraordinary degree the freshness of a child's vision—obstinate, opinionated, but always open to new findings. He maintained on principle the importance of tradition and of wise habit in literature and in life, but he was always capable of being surprised and of surprising. In this he was the exact opposite of those romantic professors of freedom whose lives so often harden in the rigid rut of their own clichés.[2]

There is a story that Lewis returned three days after his death to an old disciple perplexed by moral problems. He appeared as in life—red-faced, loud-voiced, robust—and said simply: "It's all right, you know. It's all right." Uncharacteristically unemphatic and understated: characteristically surprising. To anyone who knew and understood Lewis it has the ring of authenticity.

Sheldonian Theatre, Oxford

FROM G. K. CHESTERTON TO C. S. LEWIS

Peter Milward

Peter Milward, S.J., was educated at Wimbledon College and entered the Society of Jesus (the Jesuits) in 1943. After studying medieval philosophy at Heythrop College, he went to Oxford University in 1950 to study Classics and English Literature at Campion Hall. While there, he attended Lewis's lectures and later conducted a long correspondence with him after going to Japan in 1954. Ordained as a priest in 1960, he began teaching English literature at Sophia University in Tokyo in 1962. He is a prolific author of more than three hundred books, ranging from Shakespeare to Hopkins to Chesterton. Among his writings is A Challenge to C. S. Lewis *(Cranbury, N.J.: Associated University Presses, 1995).*

I forget when I first made the acquaintance of C. S. Lewis; but it was, no doubt, owing to his *Screwtape Letters*, which I read while I was a boy at Wimbledon. Immediately on reading, I was transformed into a fan of his, and I was always pleased to hear his book quoted, as it was so often, in our school retreats. I was also envious of the boys at our sister school in North London, Stamford Hill, where I heard one of the Jesuit fathers was using the book as his textbook for R.D. classes, albeit by an Anglican author! Soon after war broke out, I went on to read his other best-seller, *The Problem of Pain*, and his radio talks on Christianity, then published separately as *Broadcast Talks*, *Christian Behavior*, and *Beyond Personality*, and only later put together under the title of *Mere Christianity*.

It must have been my reading of these last-mentioned books that led me to relate my growing addiction to C. S. Lewis to my previous passion for G. K. Chesterton. Here was another great Christian author emerging as the leading champion of the faith in wartime England, the one on whom—for all his allegiance to another, Anglican denomination—Chesterton's mantle seemed to have fallen. It was only later, after my coming to Japan in 1954, that I learnt both from his autobiographical *Surprised by Joy* and from his posthumous *God in the Dock*, that Chesterton's writings had indeed been instrumental in his conversion from atheism to Christianity, above all *The Everlasting Man*.

My impression of Lewis's affinity with Chesterton was both deepened and enlarged when I went up to Oxford in 1950 as a Jesuit student to read the Classics. Soon after my arrival at Campion Hall for the Michaelmas Term we had a guest night to which Lewis himself had been invited by the Master, Fr. Tom Corbishley. My first impression on setting eyes on him was one of astonishment, since, for all his intellectual affinity with Chesterton, I had formed the image of Lewis as a slim, ascetic-looking man; yet here was a burly, red-faced, jovial man with an egg-head and a booming voice—and, as I later heard, no less fond of his pint of beer than of his tobacco-pipe. After all, his affinity with Chesterton extended from the mind to the body, from a witty intellect to a corpulent frame, though he was more portly than fat.

From the beginning I made a point of attending the meetings of the renowned Socratic Club over which he presided in his genial, democratic manner, leaving Miss Stella Aldwinkle to take the chair. There I could observe him every week at closer quarters and listen to his occasional interventions in the discussion, when everything he said, though all too brief, was penetrating and to the point. For the most part, he seemed to be restraining himself under extreme provocation, till he could (like the Psalmist) keep silence no longer; and then his utterances, though deferential, could be devastating. In the same way, when I changed (on my appointment for Japan) from Classical Mods to English, I made a point of attending all the lectures of "Mr. Lewis," specifically his "prolegomena" to Medieval and Renaissance literature, which were subsequently published, the former under the title of *The Discarded Image* and the latter as the lengthy introduction, "Old Learning and New Ignorance," to his learned *Oxford History of English Literature in the Sixteenth Century*. These lectures were by far the most popular of all those provided by the School of English, since the content was so fascinating, the presentation was so lucid, and the delivery so clear and considerate for note-taking students.

All this time, I had only watched and listened to Lewis from afar, as a distant admirer; but in my final year I summoned up the courage to ask him after his last lecture if I might come and see him in his rooms at Magdalen. I particularly wished to ask him about his evident interest in angels, which I had noticed in my favorite novel of his, *Out of the Silent Planet*, since I myself had a special interest in the angelology of St. Thomas. But when I visited him in his rooms at the appointed time, I was nonplussed by his opening question, "Why do you think so many Irishmen remain bachelors?" As I was thinking more of angels, it never occurred to me that this was a very personal question relating to himself as an Irishman and a bachelor. It was only long after my arrival in Japan that I came to realize how at that very time his thoughts were moving from angels in outer space to marriage with an American lady named Joy Davidman; and so when I first read his autobiography, *Surprised by Joy*, I had no inkling of the ambiguity in the title.

At the *viva* exam after my written finals in English, I found Lewis on the examining board; and it was he who opened proceedings with another question that left me nonplussed: "Would you tell us something about some minor eighteenth-century author you have read and enjoyed?" All I could say was, like Shakespeare's Cordelia, "Nothing"; and so I got off to a somewhat inauspicious start. The effect was soon counteracted when I got off to a better start for Japan, almost immediately after that *viva*, about the very time Lewis himself was starting for his new academic appointment at Magdalene College, Cambridge. Once I was in Japan, it wasn't long before I felt the prompting to renew my brief contact with Lewis by way of correspondence, first in connection with my ideas and his ideas on angels, and then with an article I was writing on his trilogy of science fiction. Thus there began between us a long, if fitful, correspondence, continuing till the very eve (if not the actual day) of his death, some items of which were published in *The Letters of C. S. Lewis*, while the originals I sent to the C. S. Lewis collection at Wheaton College, Illinois.

About this correspondence, the first thing that impressed me was the neatness and illegibility of Lewis's handwriting. His letters were a delight to look at, but a torment to decipher, till out of all the labor was born the joy of eventual enlightenment, reminding me of Christ's words about the sorrow and joy of a woman in childbirth. I felt the personality of Lewis himself in them, and I would not have had him type them for all the world! In quantity his letters were not so long—he must have had so many to write!—but in quality they were so pregnant with matter for reflection. He stated his thoughts simply and straightforwardly, even at times bluntly, as when he remarked of a certain famous Jesuit (in an unusually long letter), "I am entirely on the side of your Society for shutting de Chardin up." He could hardly have been called a Teilhardian! Another thing that impressed me about his letters was the way he invariably responded not only to my letters (even when no reply was called for) but even to my Japanese Christmas cards. He never sent me a Christmas card, as he apparently disliked the custom and (no doubt) the chore involved in this "commercialism" of Christmas, but he admired the Japanese picture of Bethlehem I had sent him, the work of the Carmelite sisters in Kyoto.

It was after my study of his science fiction that I turned to the Narnia stories, for which he has since become so famous, not least here in Japan. They confirmed me in my esteem for his powers of lucid thought and exposition as of rich and original imagination. In one of his letters to me, apropos not of these stories but of Tolkien's *The Lord of the Rings*, he referred me to his friend and colleague's important essay on fairy stories in *Essays Presented to Charles Williams*. Following his reference, I came to realize how deeply indebted both he and Tolkien must have been, not so much to *The Everlasting Man*, with its Christian view of history, as to Chesterton's *Orthodoxy*, particularly its inspiring and seminal chapter on "The Ethics of Elfland" (which I find never fails to inspire my Japanese students from year to year). In a sense, his Narnia stories may be said to be an expression of Lewis's own elfland; and insofar as they point to a moral if not a Christian allegory (for all the odd reluctance of Lewis himself to admit the fact), it is to the ethics of Elfland.

Thus it was not only as a witty apologist for Christianity in his earlier writings, but also as a deeply imaginative Christian author in his later stories, that Lewis may be seen as having taken up the prophetic mantle of Chesterton in our time. He himself, as he told me, found these stories much more congenial to his temperament than his former *Screwtape Letters*, as a result of which his name had come to be all too closely associated in the minds of his readers with that of the devil! It was as if, thanks to Narnia, he had been purified of that hellish association and raised by the power of Aslan to that heaven which is reserved for those who (like Chesterton) have become as little children. And now, I find, he is not only (as we may hope) in heaven but also in the stained-glass windows of churches in America—such as one I myself came across at St. David's Episcopal Church in Denton, Texas. It is as if "C. S. " has been transformed to "St."

LEWIS
LECTURING

Roger Poole

Roger Poole was an Exhibitioner in English at Trinity College, Cambridge, in 1958, and later a Senior Scholar and Research Scholar of the College. He attended C. S. Lewis's last series of lectures on Spenser in 1960–1961, and Lewis advised him in the matter of choosing a subject for Ph.D. research. After completing his Ph.D. studies at the University of Copenhagen, he spent three years in Paris as "lecteur" at the Sorbonne. He then received an appointment as a Lecturer in the Department of English at the University of Nottingham in 1968. He spent two periods at Yale in the 1980s as a Visiting Fellow, and in 1989 he was appointed Reader in Literary Theory at the University of Nottingham. In this chapter he shares his recollections of Lewis at Cambridge, discussing the pertinence of Lewis's approach to literature for today.

C. S. Lewis in billowing academic gown proceeding up King's Parade on a breezy Spring morning was an impressive sight. After his lecture on Spenser at the Mill Lane lecture rooms he regularly walked back to Magdalene College. Yet it was obvious that he did not feel at home in Cambridge. He moved along with his stick in one hand, books on the other arm, and his eyes focused three feet above all oncoming heads. There was a sense that he didn't expect

to meet anyone he knew and didn't want to meet anyone he didn't
know. With this self-defensive, closed gait, he seemed alienated in
Cambridge.

He was of course alienated in space, for he had come to
Cambridge to occupy a Chair that Oxford had denied him all his
life. But he was also alienated in time. Cambridge in the early sixties was full of theories Lewis disapproved of, F. R. Leavis's most of
all. Lewis was at home in a half-dozen languages and literatures, a
citizen of the medieval and Renaissance worlds, a polymath, a uni-
versalist, and two-thirds a Platonist. In the dialectic of ironies
played out between Oxford and Cambridge since 1284, the arrival
of Lewis at Cambridge was one of the most cruel.

For Lewis was anything but a Cambridge mind. I heard the last
two sets of lectures he gave: those on iconography of *The Faery
Queene* (which were published eventually as *Spenser's Images of
Life*, expertly edited from the lecture notes by Alastair Fowler), and
they were startlingly different from anything else available at
Cambridge at that time (1960). His references were to the latest
scholarship in neoplatonism: to Robert Ellrodt's *Neoplatonism in
the Early Poetry of Spenser*, to Jean Seznec's *The Survival of the
Pagan Gods*, to Edgar Wind's *Pagan Mysteries of the Renaissance*.
He was lecturing at such an altitude of abstraction that seasoned
Renaissance scholars of a much more mundane kind were seen to
snap their notebooks to with irritation. The audience as a whole
simply gaped. It was a virtuoso performance.

I have read *The Canadian C. S. Lewis Journal* since its foundation, and indeed possess a complete run of copies since its first
number in January 1979. If I presume to add my groatsworth of
wit to the many excellent and profound contributions which have
appeared over the years, it is because I have come to see Lewis as
an even more important figure for the immediate future within
"English studies" than he has been in the past. For the tradition
that he instantiated and so brilliantly performed out of, is a tradition that stands in danger of annihilation within the next ten years,
if the current educational "reforms" are allowed to be carried

through in the English universities. While I was reading the *Journal* with an eye to the past, there seemed no need for me to add my personal recollection. But looking to the future, I would like to. For what exactly was the magic element in Lewis's lecturing technique? It was the ability to ask questions no one had thought of, and to start towards an answer of them by reference to sources no one had read. It was, in other words, the exact antithesis of clear lecturing. There were many obscurities, and the audience felt itself being shoved and bustled past many things it had not time to stop and examine. Clarity, indeed, in the sense of spelling things out, explaining, waiting until the back row had caught up, was never offered. Indeed, the boot was very much on the other foot. The assumption was that only those who were committed, interested, and prepared to put a great deal of work into thinking these lectures through were really part of the audience anyway. The lectures were, without a word being said about the matter, remorselessly elitist. But it was not any shade of social or economic elitism that was in question. It was simply that the audience for Lewis was made up of two classes of people: there were those who were fascinated by the subject itself, and those who weren't. And to the latter, he had nothing to say.

To the former he had everything to say, and, as the various contributions to *The Canadian C. S. Lewis Journal* have shown over the years, to those who were fascinated by the subject itself, Lewis was generosity itself. Nothing was too much trouble for those to whom literature mattered. Those people could ask anything, and Lewis would painstakingly grant it, to the last jot and tittle. To them his generosity was inexhaustible.

The lectures were personal explorations. They transmitted a quality of urgency. In 1960 and 1961, Lewis was aware that his time was limited. He had none to waste. Important questions had to be raised. These were the questions we should devote our attention to. It was in this mood that the lectures shot off from their mark.

Lewis carried out, before an audience which was not in the least used to this kind of lecturing, a kind of act of pure attention to what Spenser's *Faery Queene* was about. He carried out, in public, a kind of inner debate about the import of the ethical iconography of Spenser's poem, but he did so within two other circles of attention. The first was the theory of reading that he was developing at the time, and which appeared as *An Experiment in Criticism* in 1961. The other was the final debate about evil and its nature which had exercised him as a Christian thinker over many years. His attention to Spenser's text was then iconographic phenomenology; within a circle of total attention to the text, an attention which refused to impose any kind of *a priori* expectation upon it; within a circle of passionate concern about the reality of evil in the world.

It was the working out of this belief, advanced in *An Experiment in Criticism*, the belief that the reader must pay total unmediated attention to the text without imposing an *a priori* theory upon it (the objection is of course to the teaching of F. R. Leavis) that gave the lectures their unexpectedness, their electrifying suddenness. Simply because Lewis was trying to read Spenser "for the very first time," he carried out an amazing set of feats of rhetorical delivery. One of them was the device of pointing out an apparently simple point which no one had noticed, but yet was crucial to the enquiry, a kind of replay of Hercule Poirot. The apparently innocent question, however, was delivered in such a way as to leave his Hastings-like audience more completely bewildered by the apparently simple point, than it had been before it became aware of it.

One of the most memorable of these Poirot moments was his acting out of his own puzzlement about the wounded dragon upon which the "false Cupid" is standing:

> A wounded dragon under him did ly,
> Whose hideous tayle his left foot did enfold,
> And with a shaft was shot through either eye,
> That no man forth might draw, ne no man remedye

"Shot through either eye" is not a phrase over which the care-less reader might bother to pause. But Lewis pulled up short. "Shot through *either* eye," he said significantly. "Now, why, through *either* eye? You see, dragons are not like us, with both eyes in *front*" (Lewis poked out his two forefingers in front of his eyes). "No, they have their eyes to the *side*," (poking with his fingers at his temples). "So it would be a remarkable shot which penetrated the dragon's head in such a way as to pass through both eyes. A remarkable arrow. Perhaps the dragon was shot with a remarkable arrow, or by a remarkable marksman?"

Such literalness left an audience which had not perhaps given much thought before to the anatomy of dragons almost dizzied. A similar example arose during the discussion of Venus and Adonis in "The Garden of Adonis." In the published version, the effect is quiet enough:

> The form-giver, in other words, is wedded to matter: *materia appetit formam.*
>
> It is, of course, unusual in mythology to have the female parent giving form while the male parent gives matter. (pp. 52–53)

But the effect in the lecture hall was quite different. Lewis, driven to the limits of his understanding by what the text nakedly demanded that he should understand, almost shouted: "Can we endure the iconographic paradox of matter as male, and form as female?" The word *endure* had all the force of Dr. Johnson's refusal to read on in his Shakespeare. This was existential reading.

"How can *Matter* be 'the father of all forms'?" he asked.

Lewis referred again and again to Nicolaus Cusanus, a medieval philosopher who "has a claim to be considered the first relativist." Lewis paused. The title of Nicolaus Cusanus' book, published in 1440, was *De docta ignorantia*. Lewis appeared, excellent Latinist as he was, to have some trouble with the correct translation of these three words. He essayed several dry runs, and then suggested, hes-itatingly: "On the ignorance to which only the learned can attain."

The audience became aware, through this hesitation, of a vast hinterland of ambiguities to which it ought to give some attention. Everything was in motion, everything had to be decided, nothing was certain. The reader of Spenser has to work, of course, with the "books of rules," the received iconographic handbooks of the period—Horapollo's heirs, Aldus, Alciati, Valeriano—but nothing must be assumed in advance; everything was to be examined anew. It was necessary to bring one's whole mind and intelligence to this reading, which would be a reading "for the very first time," a reading which was also, of course, the hundredth reading.

The reality which lay behind Lewis's lecturing technique, and upon which it so vigorously drew, is something which is now being officially willed out of existence by the quantitative theorists who are now in charge of university education. "English Literature," like all other university subjects, is being "modularized."

"Modules" of knowledge, whose quantity and extent can and must be measured, are to be bought and sold in universities which are conceived of as supermarkets. Descriptions of "modularization," now going the rounds of the British universities, make it clear that the direct aim of the process of "modularization" is the quantification of knowledge. To this end, lecturers must speak plainly, without ambiguity, in a plain and answerable style, making sure that everything is clear at all points, such that exact examining can be carried out, allowing of a scientifically accurate grading of a student's "skills."

It is precisely because Lewis himself was *not* pellucidly clear at all points, but difficult and demanding, drawing his audience on to things they had not thought about, that I (for one) remember his lectures. It was precisely because he did *not* conceive of literature in a quantitative way as a learnable "skill," that he kept redefining all his terms of reference. It was precisely because he did not think that literature could be "taught" at all (in this new, naive, self-indulgent sense of the "skills" theorists) that he kept on enquiring, both of himself and of his hearers, how it could be learnt about, entered into or existentially grasped.

My view then is that Lewis belongs not only to a past period of "English Studies," but is a necessary ally in a very proximate future. His books are there, yes, certainly, and should be re-read. But students' recollections are valuable too. It is necessary to remember, to try to analyze, in retrospect, how Lewis read, thought, and lectured. We lose Lewis's insight into the nature of *reading* at our peril. I have already mentioned his late book *An Experiment in Criticism*. While in some ways it simply does not see (is blind to) the point of Leavisian reading, it does state a necessary point of view about the nature of reading itself which is, if anything, more relevant now than it was when it appeared in 1961.

When I wrote to him to congratulate him on what was at that time seen as a very eccentric book, he replied on a postcard:

> I am delighted to hear that you approved the
> *Experiment*: all the more because I anticipate great
> unpopularity for it—unless the tide is just on the
> turn already. I may then rank as a deliverer and
> really be only a symptom.

The tide was indeed on the turn, but it was not the tide Lewis was expecting. It was the tide of literary criticism and theory, from structuralism to deconstruction, on a scale that he could not possibly have imagined.

Yet it is not, ultimately, *that* tide of literary criticism and theory (which he would so much have disliked and mistrusted) that has turned out to be the danger. The danger has turned out to be the swelling in, wave after wave, of what Lewis's great adversary called in his own last books "cock-a-hoop technologico-Benthamism." Thirty years later, "technologico-Benthamism" is more "cock-a-hoop" than ever, modularizing the teaching of English Literature and quantifying the qualitative.

What an irony, that it was F. R. Leavis who had correctly identified the real enemy of English Literature, and that C. S. Lewis, had he lived to see the educational theorizing of the 1980s, could only have become Leavis's greatest ally!

The move to Cambridge was, after all then, symptomatic. But it was symptomatic of something that, in 1961, Lewis could not possibly have foreseen, and that was that a government would arise that would seriously consider the teaching of English, or the learning of it, as a quantifiable skill. Neither of these Winston Smiths lived long enough to see the full effects of what Big Brother was capable of. But neither would have believed either, that their students and heirs could have *read* so flaccidly, and for so long, as to allow it to happen.

Magdalene College, Cambridge

SHADOWLANDS

David Graham

Shadowlands is a term Aslan used in The Last Battle *as a metaphor for the earthly realm, indicative of the limited, unenlightened view of reality that its transitory inhabitants possess. Plato's cave dwellers in his story from Book VII of* The Republic *represent a similar situation as they only have a partial and shadowy view of existence. Shadowlands is the name also given to the theatre renditions that depict Lewis's marriage to Joy Davidman. Editor David Graham here reflects on the film productions about this aspect of Lewis's life.*

> I never lost as much but twice,
> And that was in the sod;
> Twice have I stood a beggar
> Before the door of God!
> Angels—twice descending,
> Reimbursed my store—
> Burglar! Banker—Father!
> I am poor once more!
> —Emily Dickinson

It is not often that a man who spends his career as a scholar in the world of academia receives much attention from the public.

Exceptions do occur from time to time, but by and large the arenas of politics, sports, and entertainment are the vistas that produce most widely recognized individuals. With the PBS (Public Broadcasting System) television release of William Nicholson's 1985 film *Shadowlands*, followed after a few years by its stage adaptation for Broadway, then later produced as a movie for the big screen by Sir Richard Attenborough in 1993, the life of one such exception has gained more attention over the last two decades. C. S. Lewis was the one featured in these *Shadowlands* productions, not so much for his writings or his well-attended lectures or his popular broadcast talks over the BBC (British Broadcasting Corporation) as for his marriage to Joy Davidman. The PBS film (starring Joss Ackland and Claire Bloom), the play (featuring Nigel Hawthorne and Jane Lapotaire, then Jane Alexander) and the Attenborough movie (with Anthony Hopkins and Debra Winger) show the agony and the ecstasy of Lewis's falling in love with a woman dying of cancer, her recovery, their joy together, then her relapse and death, followed by Lewis's sorrow. Throughout the dramas, Lewis's Christian faith is tested and matured as he faces the pain and death of his beloved Joy.

While the productions are well done, they are nonetheless dramas—not biographies—and as such are often at variance with the factual reality of Lewis's life. In the Attenborough directed movie, for example, the discrepancies between fact and fiction abound. (1) Lewis is shown driving a car with Joy on their belated honeymoon, but in real life Lewis never succeeded in learning how to drive and was always chauffeured when he traveled. (2) The movie only shows Joy with one son, Douglas, but she really had two, as she brought both Douglas and David to England with her. (3) Lewis was at Cambridge when he married Joy, not Oxford. (4) Lewis's tutorials were to one or (after the war) two students at a time, not four (as the film depicts it.) (5) Tutorials consisted of a student reading his or her essay to Lewis, followed by critique and discussion. They were not the one-sided lecturing sessions that the movie shows. (6) Lewis was no longer giving tutorials by the time he and Joy married, nor later (with one exception) when she died. (The film shows the arrival of a new pupil after Joy's death to call him back to his daily duties, with Lewis offering his pupil the made-for-movie line, "We read to know we are not alone.") (7) The movie has Lewis going up the Magdalen Tower for the very first time in the 1950s after Joy had suggested he do so. In fact, Lewis had been walking up the tower for the better part of three decades, climbing the stairs for the annual May Day celebration (cf. Warren Lewis's diary entry for May 1, 1930, in *Brothers & Friends* or C. S. Lewis's diary entry for May 1, 1926, in *All My Road Before Me*). (8) The real Inklings were missing from the film—the only named colleague being a certain "Christopher," who was much too old to be the character of Christopher Tolkien. Where were J. R. R. Tolkien, Colin Hardie, Owen Barfield, Nevill Coghill, Humphrey Havard, David Cecil, Gervase Mathew, James Dundas-Grant, or the other real-life "Bird & Baby" patrons? (9) In one scene, Lewis is having an autographing session at Blackwell's Bookstore in Oxford. This confabulation is inconsistent with Lewis's character. (10) It was George Sayer, a former pupil, and not his brother Warren (as the movie depicts) who was with C. S. Lewis when he first met Joy Davidman. Also contrary to the movie, she did not come alone but with a friend named Phyllis Williams. Nor did the meeting take place in a hotel restaurant, but rather in Lewis's Magdalen College rooms, where they had lunch. (11) Lewis and stepson Douglas Gresham's heartfelt meeting to share their grief over Joy's death did not occur while up in the house attic, sitting by the Narnia-inspiring wardrobe, or talking about Douglas's supposed doubts about God. It was less romantic than that. In real life, Douglas was recalled from boarding school, and when he first walked through the door and into the common room at the Kilns, he saw Lewis, simply said, "Oh Jack!" and burst into tears as he and Lewis embraced. (12) Lewis's grief was more of a private affair; his public outbursts in the film about God's goodness (or lack of it) were in reality confined to paper (*A Grief Observed*). (13) Lewis is pictured as serious, somber, and later somewhat shaken in his Christian faith by Joy's illness and death. While Lewis was sincere, he was seldom solemn or morose, and although he did grieve over Joy and struggle with his concept of God, his faith remained intact. (His book *A Grief Observed*, written through the pain that followed Joy's death, was meant to be more than an anguished cry—it was something of an apologetic as well.) Those who knew Lewis (or "Jack" as he was called by friends and family) on an intimate level spoke of him as a genial, almost jolly person whose humor was often displayed even in his most serious discussions. One such friend was Sheldon Vanauken, who thought that "Winger did a good job as Joy, and CSL's brother might have been played by the Major himself. But Anthony Hopkins was never CSL. The jovial, genial, beer-drinking Lewis was never seen . . . nor the compelling lecturer, one of the best Oxford ever knew. (Why they only showed him talking to a handful of women in funny hats, I can't think.)"[1] (14) Hopkins' lecturing style and content were inaccurate—too much animation and hand-waving. Lewis's style was less dramatic and affected. The movie depicted him as memorizing one sermon and delivering the same moral platitudes over and over to different audiences, giving smug explanations for the theological problem of pain. "Pain is God's megaphone to rouse a deaf world." Yet one of the things that makes a strong impression on the Lewis reader is his variety, how little of his work (barring letters) repeats itself. As for Lewis's byline quote, it comes from his book *The Problem of Pain* (published twenty years *before* Joy died), in which he wrote,

> For that very reason there is one criticism which
> cannot be brought against me. No one can say, "He
> jests at scars who never felt a wound," for I have
> never for one moment been in a state of mind to
> which even the imagination of serious pain was less
> than intolerable. If any man is safe from the danger
> of underestimating this adversary, I am that man. I
> must add, too, that the only purpose of the book is to
> solve the intellectual problem raised by suffering; for
> the far higher task of teaching fortitude and patience

> I was never fool enough to suppose myself qualified,
> nor have I anything to offer my readers except my
> conviction that when pain is to be borne, a little
> courage helps more than much knowledge, a little
> human sympathy more than much courage, and the
> least tincture of the love of God more than all.

Indeed, Lewis himself knew how pain, suffering, and death of loved ones affected the soul. He had lost friends and family members throughout the years, from childhood when his mother died of cancer, to adult life, when he lost many friends (including his dear friend Charles Williams). Lewis's faith, however, was in the long run strengthened by these experiences, even the experience of losing his wife. They forced him to test the reality of his faith in God.

What Lewis did learn from his marriage was the full meaning of erotic love and its loss. Having successfully and brilliantly written about courtly love in his thirties as a scholarly bachelor (*The Allegory of Love*), Lewis came to understand the matter more with his heart as a happy newlywed in his fifties. "Years ago when I wrote about medieval love-poetry and described its strange, half make-believe 'religion of love,'" he states in *The Four Loves*, "I was blind enough to treat this as an almost purely literary phenomenon. I know better now. Eros by his nature invites it. Of all loves he is, at his height, most god-like; therefore most prone to demand our worship. Of himself he always tends to turn 'being in love' into a sort of religion."

"Tis better to have loved and lost than never to have loved at all," wrote Alfred Lord Tennyson. Yes it is, but why? Forrest Carter probably gave the best answer to that question in his book of Cherokee Indian memoirs entitled *The Education of Little Tree*. Little Tree described what he felt like when one of his beloved dogs died in an accident. "I felt total bad about it, and empty. Granpa said he knew how I felt, for he was feeling the same way. But Granpa said everything you lost which you had loved give you that feeling. He said the only way round it was not to love anything, which was worse because you would feel empty all the time." Indeed. Lewis, who chose to love, did grieve over Joy. Just how painful his mourning was can be seen in *A Grief Observed*. Yet he did not despair. He remained a genial man, still able to think and write and enjoy his friends, though with perhaps a deeper understanding of their own loves and bereavements. Although he might never have said so, his life after Joy did show that he felt it was truly better to have loved and lost than not to have loved at all. Perhaps something of his love for Joy is reflected by the statement he once made about a friend that he lost to death years earlier—Captain W. O. Field ("Wof"), one of several companions on his annual walking tours. "Wof was the most completely lovable man, almost, I have known. I am so glad to have known him that it almost obliterates the loss."

For all their variances from the true story of Jack and Joy Lewis, the *Shadowlands* productions are beautifully filmed, well directed, and deeply moving dramas. They show the love between a man and a woman who loved God, as well as the anguish they shared physically, emotionally, and spiritually. Death of the beloved is as sad as anything one can experience in life; yet *Shadowlands* can only tell a portion of one couple's travail. It doesn't reveal the other gift of love, the one that is still left when the beloved dies. It is a gift that grows richer and deeper with time. For along with the lingering sorrow is the blessing of a lingering love, of continued affection for the loved one and gratefulness for the love that was. For creatures who brought nothing into this world and who can carry nothing out of it, the gratefulness for having had such love is a balm for the soul when the loved one is lost. Such gratitude does at least provide a salve, especially for so deep a wound.

> To lose thee, sweeter than to gain
> All other hearts I knew.
> 'Tis true the drought is destitute,
> But then I had the dew!
> —Emily Dickinson

THE SCHOOLBOY JOHNSON

Claude Rawson

Interest in C. S. Lewis has continued to grow since his death in 1963, not just in the things he wrote but also in the life he lived. Several books of biography, commentary, and memoirs by Lewis's contemporaries have shed light on both the man and his writing. In this and the next chapter, two former Lewis pupils sample a few of them. George Sayer reviews A. N. Wilson's controversial C. S. Lewis: A Biography, *while Claude Rawson reviews Sayer's* Jack: C. S. Lewis and His Times, *Kathryn Lindskoog's* The C. S. Lewis Hoax, *and* Letters: C. S. Lewis, Don Giovanni Calabria: A Study in Friendship.

Claude Rawson is the Maynard Mack Professor of English at Yale University in New Haven, Connecticut, U.S.A. His books include Henry Fielding and the Augustan Ideal under Stress, Gulliver and the Gentle Reader, Order from Confusion Sprung: Studies in Eighteenth-Century Literature from Swift to Cowper, Satire and Sentiment: 1660–1830, *and, most recently,* The Cambridge History of Literary Criticism, volume 4: The Eighteenth Century *(with H. B. Nisbet). He is General Editor of the* Cambridge History of Literary Criticism *and Chairman of the Yale Boswell Editions. He studied English with Lewis as an undergraduate at Magdalen College, Oxford, from October 1952 to December 1954, when Lewis left for Cambridge, and remained in*

occasional contact with him after that. He wrote Stephen Schofield
following an inquiry about his memories of Lewis. "I'm not a Lewis
specialist in any sense, though I have a strong awareness of his
example and the power of his personality. I was too young to get the
most out of the experience of my weekly tutorial with him; and my
memories tally with those of Norman Bradshaw [a Lewis pupil
from the 1930s] about his "bullying" style. I also vividly knew
Lewis's generosity." His review of the aforementioned books was
published in The Times Literary Supplement, *August 11–17, 1989.*

When Roy Campbell discovered in 1927 that his wife was having an affair with Vita Sackville-West, he told C. S. Lewis about it
in a London pub. Lewis "listened in fascinated silence" and finally
said: "Fancy being cuckolded by a woman!" The remark threw
Campbell into a "black rage" of wounded pride which seems to
have lingered for years, though Lewis probably had no thought of
giving pain. But there was nothing uncharacteristic about his
response. It comes over with a note of ribaldry, simultaneously
bluff and bookish, which was especially his own. *Cuckold* was a
favorite Lewis word, and I have never heard it spoken so often as
during the two and a half years I was an undergraduate pupil of his
in the 1950s. It is not (and I suspect wasn't in 1927) a usual or
merely functional usage. The predicament it nowadays evokes is a
literary one, the kind that is jeered at in comedy or precipitates
crises of honor in more elevated genres, rather than the real-life
phenomenon of conjugal infidelity and distress to which we
respond when it happens around us, and to which we don't
instinctively apply that particular term. Lewis was in principle alive
to the distinction, especially when it came to writing sensitive letters of advice to a correspondent who faced marital breakdown.
But he took a donnish pleasure in situations which seemed
reducible to literary stereotype; and in contexts unencumbered by
the obligation to give comfort, in the largely male rituals of pub or
tutorial, he tended or pretended to see comedy, rather than pathos

or pathology, in the sexual travails of others. And his conception of sexual comedy was schoolmasterly as well as bookish. He rejoiced in one of his pupils' unwitting description of courtly love as "a vast medieval erection," and in the praise by a Bishop of Exeter of a girls' school production of *A Midsummer Night's Dream*: "I was very interested in seeing for the first time in my life a female Bottom."

This colors a good deal of his work as a critic: both the characteristic gusto of his reports on his reading, and his admonitions on how we should regulate our own. It explains, at least partly, the remark in his essay on Addison (one of the very best among his shorter critical works) about the scatological passages in Swift and Pope: "even their love of filth is, in my opinion, much better understood by schoolboys than by psychoanalysts: if there is something sinister in it, there is also an element of high-spirited rowdiness." The recognition of "something sinister" is more than perfunctory. Lewis tells us that "rage, exasperation, and something like despair are never far away" from the humor. But his main impulse is to assert the "high-spirited rowdiness." The mythologized schoolboy world that it evokes is in many ways an affectionate displacement of the companionships of his adult life, especially among the Inklings, where, we are told, the wit and brilliance tended to become "riotous": "no sound delights me more," his brother reports him as saying, "than male laughter." But there is also the pedagogue's warning, conspiratorial and knowing about schoolboy ways, and in its fashion perhaps more starchy than frivolous, that the psychoanalytic perspective is getting it wrong, even as he concedes "sinister" undertones and offers no alternative way of disposing of them.

The promotion of schoolboy fun cannot be separated from the fact that Lewis's own schooldays were no paradise of carefree "rowdiness." None of his school experiences seems to have been very happy, and the memory rankled. In his autobiography *Surprised by Joy* he called one of his schools Belsen. He only lasted a year at Malvern (alias Wyvern), about which he wrote some of the most

ferocious pages in that book. (By a queer symmetry of fate, his latest biographer, George Sayer, who was an undergraduate pupil of
his, went on to become the senior English master at the same
school.) "I sometimes wonder", he once wrote, "if this country will
kill the public schools before they kill it . . . . I really don't know
what gifts the public schools bestow . . . unless contempt of the
things of the intellect, extravagance, insolence, self-sufficiency, and
sexual perversion are to be called gifts." His characteristic nostalgia
was for a childhood idyll that excluded or preceded school, for the
old happy companionship with his brother, the pleasures of their
fantasy world of Boxen, the sense of imaginative freedom tinged
with the menace of school. The two brothers returned to this
world when they could, despite Warren's alcoholic upheavals and
other sadnesses, and Sayer cites a moving account by Warren
(himself an impressively gifted writer) of Lewis's last days: "Again
we were together in a new 'little end room,' shutting out from our
talk the ever present knowledge that as in the black years of Belsen,
the holidays were drawing swiftly to a close and a new term fraught
with unknown possibilities awaited both of us."

These survivals of boyhood may have contributed to his success as a children's writer and doubtless explain his slightly prig-
gish view "that a children's story which is enjoyed only by children
is a bad children's story." It is surprising how many of Lewis's most
characteristic adult guises, including his famous habit of
"Johnsonian" repartee, originated in early childhood. At the age of
eight, returning from a holiday in France, he announced that he
had "a prejudice against the French." When his father asked why, he
replied, "If I knew why, it would not be a prejudice." The name
"Jack," by which Lewis was known to his friends and which is so
well suited to his jovial "beer and Beowulf" image, was inaugurated in an imperious announcement at around the age of four
that he would only answer to the name "Jacksie." There were
doubtless harder forenames for a small boy to bear than Clive
Staples, but Lewis retained a child's awareness of a name's baleful
power and began one of his Narnia books with "There was a boy

called Eustace Clarence Scrubb, and he almost deserved it. His parents called him Eustace Clarence and his schoolmasters called him Scrubb. I can't tell you how his friends spoke to him, for he had none."

Humphrey Carpenter, who has written best (in his book *The Inklings*, 1978) on the schoolboy survival in Lewis, perceptively sees in the adult novel *That Hideous Strength* a working out of Lewis's "schoolboy resentment of bullies." If that book anatomizes the schoolboy gang in its sinister college-committee and State-totalitarian extensions, the passage about young Scrubb expresses some playful collusive assent to the gang ethic. Lewis's enduring delight in the worlds of epic and saga almost certainly included a sense of their deep analogy with what Horace Walpole called the "mimic republic" of schoolboys. The schoolboy aspect of heroic codes of prowess in battle, game, and conspiracy, which Isherwood and Auden half-admiringly recognized in the sagas but also perceived as a component of Fascism, held an equal (and equally ambivalent) fascination for Lewis. Among the books reread in his last days, with their bittersweet sense of "holidays . . . drawing swiftly to a close," was the *Iliad*, which Lewis reported enjoying "more than I have ever done." His love of Homer was richer and deeper than any schoolboy taste for adventure, but it is not unconnected with his lifelong predilection for the adventure stories of Rider Haggard and others. "That something," he wrote in 1947, "which the educated receive from poetry can reach the masses through stories of adventure, and almost in no other way." Homer, Haggard, and science fiction, though he did not "think them of equal literary merit," are frequently mentioned by him as offering similar satisfactions. He told Arthur Greeves in 1932 that when he wanted light reading, he wanted "not so much a grown-up 'light' book (to me usually the hardest of all kinds of reading) as a boy's book." Carpenter notes the self-conscious presence of Edwardian schoolboy slang in his literary judgments: "he called one author 'a corking good writer,' another story 'a tip-top yarn,' and yet another 'an absolute corker.'"

"Psychoanalysts" will doubtless have their own say about all this: the sense of tribal horrors, the nostalgia for boyhood, the reading tastes, and the bluff defiance of psychoanalysts in the name of sturdy schoolboy sense. If so, they might or might not be surprised to find Lewis ready to agree with them. As Sayer makes evident in his biography, *Jack*, Lewis was plagued from his schooldays with sadomasochistic fantasies which "caused him great psychic pain," though the more youthful of his letters to his friend Arthur Greeves, collected in *They Stand Together* (1979), report these fantasies in tones of relaxed connoisseurship:

> "Across my knee" of course makes one think of positions for Whipping: or rather not for whipping (you couldn't get any swing) but for that torture with brushes. This position, with its childish, nursery association would have something beautifully intimate and also very humiliating for the victim.

He informed Greeves that loving the rod as he (but not Greeves) did had "a poignant sensual side and a vague sentimental side," just like "normal desire," and that Rousseau, *qui avait, lui aussi, un penchant pour la verge*, differed in some respects from himself: "His taste is altogether for suffering rather than inflicting: which I can feel too, but it is a feeling more proper to the other sex." (He described the *Confessions* as "altogether a 'really rather lovely' book.") Lewis's fantasies were heterosexual, whereas Greeves was homosexual without sadomasochistic leanings: "you are interested in a brand of *That* which doesn't appeal to me, and I in one that doesn't appeal to you."

This sounds pretty self-possessed. But Greeves was perhaps the one person with whom he could discuss *That* with such apparent ease (Greeves deleted all such passages before he died, and they have been photographically restored). Sayer reports that even Lewis's schoolboy reading was colored by what he himself thought of as pathological elements. His interest in science fiction and space-travel, already in evidence, was hardly a hedonistic surrender to the pleasures of imagined worlds. "It was an intense passion that made him feel almost drunk, a passion he describes as a coarse, heady attraction to be exorcised, more a lust than a genuine imaginative experience, and an affair for the psychoanalysts to explain."

The world of the schoolboy and that of the psychoanalyst were thus not as distinct as they might seem from the remark about the satirists. Behind the breeziness, Lewis was always aware of his own oddities as potentially within the psychiatrists' purview. He and Sayer once went into an inn dressed in shabby walking clothes. The landlady had "gentry staying in the house" and didn't want them to see the poorly dressed pair. She said that if they had money and would wipe their feet properly, she would give them a plate of cold meat in the back kitchen. Lewis "took it like a lamb. He actually took his shoes off before entering and . . . whispered: 'You know I enjoy being ordered about like this. What would the psychologists make of it?'" In this, as in other respects, he resembled Samuel Johnson, who liked to be "scolded" and "governed." I think he was almost certainly conscious of this and felt a certain pride in it.

In the 1920s, Lewis took a fashionable interest in Freud and was for a time "eager to analyze himself and his friends in terms of the 'latest perversions.'" He sometimes felt that this fascination, like his interest in the occult, was "morbid," and he satirized psychoanalysis along with free verse and modernism in that stodgiest of his fictions, *The Pilgrim's Regress* (1933). His lecture "Psycho-Analysis and Literary Criticism" (published in 1942 but delivered earlier) is pompous, labored, and triumphally obtuse in his most hectoring style. But he also confessed in a letter of 1940 that his views were colored by "a partly pathological hostility to what is fashionable" and that he "may therefore have been betrayed into statements on this subject which I am not prepared to defend." Like many literary people, he retained a liking for Jung when he rejected Freud. He took an informed interest in the philosophical aspects of psychoanalysis and in its implications for Christian thought, and at a very early stage made thoughtful distinctions between repression and "self-control." Few people who heard his dismissive outbursts against psychiatry realized how close his own daily life was to people who had need of it, including his own brother, who had periodic bouts of alcoholism, and Dr. Askins, the brother of Mrs. Moore (the older woman Lewis lived with on terms that are still unclear), who suffered from "war neurasthenia."

The reductiveness with which he reacted to psychiatric doctrines had about it a quality of Johnsonian overkill. This included, as often with Johnson, a sense that the realities were too complex to be allayed by his own flattening statements, and a feeling above all of his own vulnerability. This shows very clearly in Lewis's report to Greeves of Askin's case. Askin's psychiatrist told Lewis that "every neurotic case went back to childish fears of the father," and Sayer says the only Freudian teaching he valued was that which dealt with "the relationship of parents and children" (what other kind was there?). You can sense the potential for Lewisian ribaldry as he warned Greeves: "whatever you do never allow yourself to get a neurosis." But this modulates quickly into a sober reflection that "You and I are both qualified for it, because we were both afraid of our fathers as children." And whatever jeering there might have been at psychoanalytic theory, there is a humble recognition of the value of practical therapy as he passed on to Greeves the psychiatrist's advice to avoid introspection and brooding: "Keep to work and sanity and open air . . . . We hold our mental health by a thread, and nothing is worth risking for it. Above all, beware of excessive daydreaming." The sentiments are again highly Johnsonian, and studiedly so.

Lewis was a lifelong reader of Boswell, whose *Life of Johnson* he identified in boyhood as a book to read at meals, the kind of "gossipy, formless book which can be opened anywhere." For Boswell himself, he seems to have had an affectionate contempt that was appropriate to the case. In 1921 he described his statue in the market square at Lichfield as the "masterpiece of comic or satiric statuary. It represents a little eighteenth-century gentleman with a toy sword": and he marveled at "how cunningly a kind of simpering

modesty is combined with a sort of profound vanity in this figure."
But in Johnson, Lewis found a model for a whole range of behavior patterns, from insatiable tea drinking to "talking for victory."
The most quintessentially Lewisian sentiments or idiosyncrasies, even when not especially Johnsonian in character, are often conceived or presented under cover of a Johnsonian *mot*, and a deep self-implicating affection for Johnson is sensed even in ostensibly negative contexts. In the splendid account of John Knox in *English Literature in the Sixteenth Century*, Lewis cites an example of self-deception in Knox, adding: "no equal instance of self-ignorance is recorded until the moment at which Johnson pronounced himself 'a very polite man.'" I suspect that Lewis liked to imagine himself (burly, forthright, untidy, inwardly tormented) as not "a very polite man" in exactly the way in which he thought Johnson wasn't.

All his life he cited Johnson as a source of wisdom, a guide to attitudes, a trigger for debate. His habitual "talking for victory" may have begun very young, but it was undoubtedly colored by Johnson's example, and his brother Warnie used the Johnsonian phrase to describe it. The practice became something of a sport among Lewis's friends, doubtless prodded by his competitive example, and it frequently showed itself in a strain of triumphalist high spirits in his tutorial manner. Those victories were easy ones. Sayer insists that there was "nothing of the bully" in that context, but those who remember otherwise will find alternative accounts in the rival biographies. (Sayer's recollections are almost twenty years earlier than mine.)

Lewis admired other victorious talkers and masters of the pregnant phrase or knockdown paradox, and especially Chesterton, whom he mentioned alongside Johnson among his major influences. But he hated Macaulay:

> It's not the style that's the trouble; it's a very
> good style within its own limits. But the man is a
> humbug—a vulgar, shallow, self-satisfied mind,
> absolutely inaccessible to the complexities and deli-
> cacies of the real world. He has the journalist's air of

being a specialist in everything, of taking in all
points of view, and being always on the side of the
angels: he merely annoys a reader who has had the
least experience of *knowing* things, of what knowing
is like. There is not two pence worth of real thought
or real nobility in him. But he isn't dull . . . .

It is possible here also to see an element of self-implication. The
"very good style within its own limits" is seen, as Lewis's own style
has sometimes been seen, as reductive of "the complexities and
delicacies of the real world." The same might be said of Chesterton,
and it is not always easy to predict, among writers whom Lewis
resembled, whether he would be attracted or repelled by what they
had in common. But Johnson was special and what Lewis loved in
him was more than conversational prowess or eloquent phrase-
making. What he honored in Johnson were not only virtuosities of
definition but also a literalness which conceded precisely those
realities which fell outside the pithy formulations or explosions of
prejudice, and which Macaulay is seen as having missed. The
Johnson who despised Sterne, but who, when Goldsmith toady-
ingly referred to him as "a very dull fellow," replied, "Why, no, Sir,"
is the one who was most attractive to Lewis, and I think Johnson's
retort, in that wonderful Boswellian scene, probably lies behind the
afterthought to the tirade against Macaulay: "But he isn't dull."

The comments on Macaulay, from a diary entry in 1924, have
the forcefulness of Lewis's best critical prose. In general Lewis's letters, even in the truncated state to which some of them have been
reduced in print, contain some of his most vivid writing on both
people and books. An early example is the portrait of the English
language examiner at his viva, which is as good as Smollett: "a foul
creature, yawning insolently at his victims and rubbing his small
puffy eyes. He had the face of a pork butcher and the manners of
a village boy on a Sunday afternoon, when he has grown bored but
not yet quite arrived at the quarrelsome stage." Some of his most
arresting comments are in moments of sympathy with writers he

mainly disliked, like Sartre: "an artist in French prose" with "a sort of wintry grandeur which partly explains his immense influence." In a late *rapprochement* with Eliot, he declined the latter's invitation to comment on the New English Bible, adding: "Odd, the way the less the Bible is read, the more it is translated." Such things come over with a thrusting vivid informality, but they contain the essential quality of his critical thinking. His formal works of criticism are often elaborate orchestrations of this kind of arresting paradox or willfully surprising perspective: the attack on the Humanists in *English Literature in the Sixteenth Century* ("New Learning and New Ignorance"), the view in *The Discarded Image* of the Middle Ages as an age of systems ("Of all our modern inventions I suspect that they would most have admired the card index"), the argument that Addison's late neglect reflects the extent to which his influence has been assimilated and is a measure of the success of his "undertaking." The latter view partly derives from Johnson, and Lewis's distinction as a critic resembles Johnson's in that it is often at its most vitalizing when what it proposes seems eccentric or borders on untenability. Many have found fault or expressed radical disagreement with his first and most famous scholarly book, *The Allegory of Love*, but few have come away from it with their sense of literary history unaltered.

Sayer's book is more concerned with the life than with the work. It does not, strictly speaking, contribute a great deal of new information. Some of his personal memories of Lewis appear for the first time, and his perspective as a close friend has value. He knew Lewis well, as well perhaps as Roger Lancelyn Green and much better than Walter Hooper, whose joint biography of Lewis is agreeably supplemented but not altogether superseded by his book. On certain matters, Humphrey Carpenter's *The Inklings* offers fuller and more vivid information: not just on the coterie of which Lewis was the presiding genius, but on specific biographical matters, notably his relationship with Charles Williams and with Tolkien. But Sayer's honest and slightly plodding narrative is nevertheless an engaging addition to the record.

Kathryn Lindskoog's *The C. S. Lewis Hoax* (the latest of several books on Lewis by that author) raises doubts about the authenticity of some of Lewis's posthumous works (especially *The Dark Tower*), and about Walter Hooper's claims to intimacy with Lewis and his integrity as an editor of the master. There sometimes seems to be a case to answer, and the evidence will doubtless be clarified by more capable hands than mine (and I suspect hers).[1] But there are moments when her sleuthing produces results that are close to self-parody. She is so determined to show that Hooper was determined to show that Lewis was homosexual, that she sees a sinister motive in the fact that his edition of Lewis's correspondence with Arthur Greeves is called *They Stand Together*, which anonymous informants assure her is a "little-known homosexual euphemism": she is still trying to "locate anyone willing to be cited on the topic in a footnote." (One reviewer pointed out that the phrase comes from *Surprised by Joy*). Moreover, the cover of the book shows the two men "flanking a sketch of Oxford's Magdalen Tower, which thrusts up between them." Since Magdalen Tower is connected with Lewis but not with Greeves, she regards its presence as "illogical" except as a deliberate intimation of sins that dare not speak their name.

I hope she won't decide to turn her attention to the recently published *Letters* of C. S. Lewis and Don Giovanni Calabria (1873–1954). Father Calabria was a saintly man who founded an orphanage and later a congregation of Poor Servants of Divine Providence, and who was beatified by Pope John Paul in 1988. He had lifelong ecumenical interests, reaching out to both Jews and Protestants, and he first wrote to Lewis (in Latin) in 1947 after reading an Italian translation of *The Screwtape Letters*. There are twenty-eight surviving letters amiably exchanging sentiments on spiritual and personal matters, and principally of interest perhaps because they enacted an aspiration frequently voiced by Lewis for a Europe united by a common learned language which he felt the humanists had killed: "If only that plaguey 'Renaissance' which the Humanists brought about had not destroyed Latin (and destroyed it just when they were pluming themselves that they were reviving it), we should then still be able to correspond with the whole of Europe." Martin Moynihan, who has produced a bilingual text, speaks well of this "characteristic tilt at the Renaissance and especially its destruction of everyday Latin in favor of a forced Classicism. In the battle between 'Trojans' and 'Greeks,' Lewis was always with the Trojans, with the so-called dunces against the so-called humanists, with the true romantics, that is, against the false classicists."

Only a few of Father Calabria's letters to Lewis remain, because of Lewis's custom of burning letters two days after he received them. This was, he explained to Don Luigi Pedrollo, a member of Calabria's congregation, not because he didn't value them, but because he didn't wish "things often worthy of sacred silence" to be read by posterity: "For nowadays inquisitive researchers dig out all our affairs and besmirch them with the poison of 'publicity.'" This was not simply a hostility to journalistic investigators. Lewis rarely kept letters, including letters from T. S. Eliot and Charles Williams. He also discarded many of his own manuscripts, and for a long time failed even to date his letters, a fact which he came to regret. Part of this was probably casual habit. But he disliked not only journalistic prying, but also the kind of literary criticism which dealt in biographical personality, and was resolutely opposed to "research" and its increasing encroachment on the institutional study of literature. Sayer repeats his now familiar quip that "there were three kinds of literacy at Oxford: the literate, the illiterate, and the B. Litterate, and that personally he preferred the first two." In 1955 or 1956 I wrote to him about my own incipient B. Litt. "research" (on a topic quite unconnected with him), and men-tioned a rumor, then likely to strike anyone as unusual, that a woman then visiting London was doing research on himself. I remember receiving a characteristically laconic reply to the effect that he would hate to be pursuing either my research topic or hers. Perhaps the lady was Kathryn Lindskoog, who had a summer school scholarship at the University of London around the time, according to the dustjacket of *The C. S. Lewis Hoax.*

C. S. LEWIS AND ADULTERY

George Sayer

George Sayer was Lewis's pupil while reading English at Magdalen College, Oxford, in the 1930s. This was the beginning of a friendship that was to last until Lewis's death in 1963. In 1988 Sayer's biography of Lewis, Jack: C. S. Lewis and His Times, *was published. Two years later another biography of Lewis was released, this one by the novelist A. N. Wilson, bearing the simple title* C. S. Lewis: A Biography. *Wilson's book generated a good bit of controversy when published, with many praising it and not a few censuring it. Certainly no one who read the book seemed indifferent to it. A number of reviews came from both sides of the Atlantic. Perhaps the most insightful and balanced came from Sayer, who was able to point out both merits and demerits in Wilson's approach. This article was originally printed in* Crisis *in November 1990, being modified somewhat for inclusion in his new afterword of the second edition of* Jack, *which came out in 1994.*

A. N. Wilson has all the biographer's gifts. He is learned, intelligent, and witty, with a gift for spotting interesting and unusual facts and traits of character. As he even writes fluently and often amusingly, he is rarely dull. His *Tolstoy*, the biography published just before *C. S. Lewis*, was also scholarly. It shows a remarkable grasp of the complex and voluminous source material, most of it in Russian—he worked on it for fourteen years and learned Russian in order to get to grips with it. His *Hilaire Belloc* was a most entertaining book, and I think an understanding one. When I heard that Collins, the British publishers, had commissioned Wilson to write a biography of Lewis, I thought it an admirable choice, especially as he had taught English at New College, Oxford; was, like Lewis, a member of the Church of England; and had had some training in theology.

Here, I thought, was just the man to make use of the material that was not available when I wrote my book, or that I was not permitted to use, such as Joy Davidman's letters, the oral histories and accounts of Lewis recorded and assembled at the Wade Center in Wheaton, Lewis's diary, and perhaps even some of the many annotations to be found in the books of his library. I thought Wilson should also be just the man to assess Lewis as theologian, literary critic, and novelist—for he himself is the author of ten novels. Perhaps this last activity conceals a warning, for he tells us somewhere in his *Tolstoy* that in his understanding the biographer stands closer to the novelist than the chronicler. Such a writer, he maintains, cannot help falsifying.

Yet in spite of these expectations I almost refused to read the book when it appeared because many of the reviews in the London press almost amounted to a campaign of defamation of Lewis's character. Lewis was described as an adulterer twice over, a sadomasochistic pervert, a boozer, and a loud-mouthed bully. I am glad to be able to report that such reviews are not Wilson's fault. His book deserves far better, or at least more balanced, reviews than it has received. Though it is not as scholarly as *Tolstoy* was, perhaps not even as *Hilaire Belloc* was, it nonetheless has great merits.

The most obvious is its readability. It is a good piece of narrative, enlivened with sharp observation, neat vignettes of character, bizarre incidents, and quite a lot of humor. For some of this the comic novelist is responsible. Thus in describing his visit to the

Wade Center at Wheaton College, Wilson writes: "Here the faithful may see Muggeridge's portable typewriter kept, like the body of Lenin, in a glass case." Excellent fooling, but untrue. I am assured by the Director of the Center that Malcolm Muggeridge's typewriter is not and has never been there. Does this inaccuracy matter? If you think it does, perhaps you had better avoid books by biographers of the Wilson school.

He gives us lively portraits of many of the people who influenced or had much to do with Lewis, and in doing so he often finds for us material not in the other biographies. Thus he makes of Lewis's father, Albert, a grand comic character with his eccentricities and fund of splendidly told improbable stories, but he presents him as pathetic, too, "a fundamentally serious man . . . doomed to be regarded as a figure of fun by those whom he loved best."

He gives an admirable account of Mrs. Moore, the exacting lady with whom Lewis for many years shared house as the result of a rash promise made to her son before they were sent to fight on the Western Front. Without underrating her faults and the multiplicity of household tasks that she imposed on Lewis, he shows her as a generous, warm-hearted Irishwoman, just the sort whom a romantic young poet, homesick and motherless, could easily love. "Much of the shopping and fetching was only necessary because she wanted to entertain and to give people meals. Children and animals loved her. She was spontaneously affectionate."

Wilson illustrates this with the beautiful story of the occasion when she was called to do jury service in Oxford. She was found not where she should have been, inside the courtroom, but in the corridor outside, with her arm round the defendant, comforting him. Wilson, who is good at linking people and events in Lewis's life with scenes and characters in his books, suggests that Lewis had her in mind when he wrote the vision of the lady in *The Great Divorce*: "Every young man or boy that met her became her son—even if it was only the boy that brought the meat to the back door . . . every bird and beast that came near her had its place in her love. In her they became themselves."

Wilson shows the importance to Lewis of his friends in the accounts of his relationships with Tolkien, Hugo Dyson, and Charles Williams, three most complex characters, the first two of whom had much to do with Lewis's conversion. He is informative on the subject of Tolkien, perhaps at one time Lewis's closest friend, and their lengthy discussions about the Oxford English school, myth, and their own writings. Without Lewis, Tolkien would probably never have completed *The Lord of the Rings* and without Tolkien, Lewis would probably never have thought of writing *Out of the Silent Planet*. The friendship cooled in later years. Tolkien was disappointed that Lewis never became a Roman Catholic, was intolerant of Charles Williams, and repelled by Joy Davidman, whom Lewis married a few years before her death.

The pages on Williams seem to me successful. They include a helpful discussion of *The Place of the Lion*, the book that brought Williams to Lewis's notice, but surprisingly nothing about Williams's poetry, to which Lewis devoted a whole book. Perhaps Wilson thinks it as bad as he thinks Lewis's own poetry.

The portrait of Joy is unsympathetic, but not, I think, on the whole unfair, although there is one occasion when, with the novelist in charge, he makes her out to be cruder and more peremptory than she was. Lady Dunbar (née Maureen Moore, Mrs. Moore's daughter) told me that she went up to Oxford to visit Joy who, now married to Lewis, was living in the Kilns and recovering from massive surgery for cancer. They went for a drive in the countryside, just the two of them alone in the car. In the course of it Joy asked her if she would give up her right to the house after the death of the brothers. Wilson's account, however, rearranges matters by setting the conversation in the house and bringing Lewis on to the scene:

"When I die and Jack dies, this house will belong to the boys."

Maureen faltered. "I think not. . . . You see, by the terms of my mother's will . . ."

"You evidently did not hear what I said," said Joy very firmly. "This house belongs to me and the boys."

"I think if you asked Jack—" Maureen began.

"I've told Jack," said Joy, looking at her shame-faced silent husband.

Lady Dunbar, with whom I have discussed it, agrees that this is an inaccurate account. It is very amusing, but the novelist does more than emphasize the go-getter in Joy; more seriously, he demeans Lewis.

Nevertheless, if the treatment of Lewis himself had been on the whole as good as that of the other characters, and Wilson's pages on some of the books, I should have little but praise for Wilson's biography. Unfortunately, it is seriously flawed, and in one vital respect wrongheaded. This is his belief that Lewis and Joy had sexual intercourse before the Christian marriage that took place in the hospital. This is a most important matter; if it is true, it shatters Lewis's credibility as an honest man and a Christian moralist. For Lewis not only taught and believed that sexual intercourse outside marriage was utterly wrong for the Christian, he told his brother and a few of his closest friends (I had the honor to be among them) that the registry office marriage was a formality to enable Joy to stay permanently in England and that any living together as man and wife was out of the question. If at the time of such statements he was making love with Joy, he would have been a contemptible liar and a hypocrite. But I am sure that those who knew of the secret marriage, and indeed all his friends, had no doubt that he was an honest man who practiced what he preached.

To support his theory of Lewis's adultery, Wilson tells us that Douglas Gresham, in an oral interview taped at the Wade Center, states that in 1955, when he was only eight, he surprised his mother and Lewis in a compromising position in her bedroom. But Gresham has stated in writing that he never made this statement, and I have it on the authority of the former curator of the Wade Center, Lyle Dorsett, that Douglas's statement is not on the tape or in the typewritten transcript that was made from it.

Wilson also claims support from an account given in my biography *Jack* of a conversation I had with Dr. Humphrey Havard several years after Lewis died, following publication of the Green-Hooper biography in 1973. I asked Dr. Havard if he thought the marriage had been consummated. Dr. Havard recollected that some time after the Christian marriage, Lewis had asked him if it was possible for a man of his age and state of health to have sexual intercourse. Wilson quite without justification places the conversation before the Christian ceremony. But in my account I make it quite clear that Lewis's conversation with Dr. Havard took place in 1958, a year after the marriage in Churchill Hospital. As this clearly took place after the marriage, it is an argument *against* his theory. Lewis would not have asked Havard about his ability to perform the sexual act after the marriage if he had been having intercourse with Joy beforehand.

Wilson also quotes a statement made by Father Bide, who performed the ceremony of the Christian marriage, in the hospital in 1956: "Joy desperately wanted to solemnize her marriage before God, and to claim the grace of the sacrament before she died." But this does not mean, as he supposes, that, smitten with guilt because of her adultery, she had virtuously and correctly not been receiving the sacrament of the Eucharist. It means rather that she desired another sacrament, that of matrimony, and therefore offers no support for Wilson's theory.

His view also seems to me to be psychologically improbable. If they had been living as man and wife after the registry office marriage, the assertive go-getter in Joy would never have tolerated the situation. She would have clamored for her rights and insisted on being given her proper social status as Mrs. C. S. Lewis.

Though Wilson depicts, sometimes rather well, most aspects of Lewis, the composite figure does not add up. I, who knew Lewis for twenty-nine years, as pupil and then as friend, find it at times almost unrecognizable. He is presented as a rather unhappy, guilt-ridden creature, obsessed with sadomasochistic fantasies, who often sought relief from his inner conflicts and uncertainties in an overly dogmatic faith, in bullying argument and, at times, even in deep drinking and bawdy talk.

For Lewis, the sexual fantasies were only a problem in the early part of his life. Overcoming them was one of the blessings he owed to his conversion. "That sort of thought," he once said, "can be fairly easily overcome by prayer and what they called 'fasting.'" I also agree with his longtime friend Owen Barfield that in his maturity he was not introspective at all. He was usually cheerful and took spontaneous, almost boyish delight in many things. He was great fun, an extremely witty and amusing companion. He was courteous and considerate to those he was with and seemed more concerned with the welfare of his friends than with himself. Although he enjoyed lively hammer-and-tongs argument, and in the heat of the argument could be insensitive to the feelings of his opponent, I never knew him to bully. He would often refrain from attacking a man whom he thought could not stand up to him. I will give one example. He went to a lecture by the well-known poet and critic Sir Herbert Read, with whose ideas he strongly disagreed. I invited him to meet Read afterwards over a glass of port or a cup of tea. I expected a lively argument. But there was nothing. Only pleasant small talk. "I didn't say what I thought," Lewis said later, "because I thought he looked unwell. It would have been unfair."

I did not much care for his end-of-term parties, but in my day they were not, as Wilson states, events at which the object was to get drunk.[1] Nor do I remember obscenities.[2] It was hard to be much in Lewis's company without being aware of his goodness, even holiness. It was nourished by prayer—he meditated daily on verses from the New Testament—by his openness to mystical experience, and his habit of communing with nature. He took his religious duties seriously, though, without ever losing his glorious sense of humor. One of these duties, he thought, was to evangelize, so

. . . Christes lore, and his apostles twelve,
He taughte, and first he folwed it himselve.

SURPRISED BY SHADOWLANDS

Philip Yancey

Philip Yancey is an editor for Christianity Today *as well as co-chair of the editorial board for* Books & Culture. *He graduated from Columbia Bible College in South Carolina and earned his M.A. from Wheaton College in Illinois, after which he worked on the staff of* Campus Life *magazine while continuing his work as a freelance journalist. His articles have appeared in many magazines, including* The Saturday Evening Post, Chicago Tribune Magazine, *and* Reader's Digest. *Several of his books have won the Gold Medallion Book of the Year Award, including* What's So Amazing about Grace?, The Jesus I Never Knew, Where Is God When It Hurts? Disappointment with God, *the* NIV Student Bible *(with cohort Tim Stafford) and his three books co-authored with Paul Brand:* Fearfully and Wonderfully Made, In His Image, *and* Pain: The Gift Nobody Wants. *After growing up in the southeastern U.S., he lived in the Chicago area for more than two decades before moving to Colorado, where he and his wife Janet now make their home. A longtime Lewis reader, Yancey here shares his reflections about the 1993 film* Shadowlands. *This article, reprinted by permission, first appeared in the April 4, 1994, issue of* Christianity Today, *the title being an allusion to Lewis's spiritual autobiography* Surprised by Joy.

Imagine my surprise at finding a theater packed with patrons awaiting the matinee showing of Richard Attenborough's *Shadowlands*. Did these people know what they would see—a film with no violence, no naked flesh, no dirty jokes, and not even a swear word, a film whose main character prays, believes in heaven, and lectures on theology?

Some evangelicals will complain that the movie distorts Lewis's life and waters down his Christian message. True, in some ways the producers settled for the Hollywood formula of a tearjerker love story played by name stars (Debra Winger and Anthony Hopkins). But let's not be too harsh: these stars speak substantive dialogue to each other—about spiritual matters, no less.

The plot line: a repressed, clubby Oxford don, accustomed to winning all arguments and dominating his private (masculine) world, finds that airtight world invaded by a brash Noo Yawker. Joy Davidman Gresham, sassy, divorced, Jewish, and a former Communist, represents everything Lewis is not. The encounter "humanizes" Lewis, bringing him first acute happiness and then acute despair. Gresham, it turns out, is dying of cancer.

"You never know how much you really believe anything until its truth or falsehood becomes a matter of life and death to you," wrote Lewis. As he sat at the bedside of the dying woman, now his wife, suddenly everything became a matter of life and death. Especially his faith.

"Drippings of Grace"

I enjoyed *Shadowlands* immensely, and I hesitate to carp about a fine film that is spurring a renewed interest in C. S. Lewis's writings. Yet readers may note that the film subtly misconstrues Lewis's views of pleasure and pain.

Several times the film repeats a scene from his lectures. We humans are not put on earth to experience happiness, Lewis declaims; that remains for another world. Lewis hammers home his ideas with percussive force even as the unfolding plot makes a conspicuous counterpoint: beyond the walls of the lecture hall, Joy is bringing him the happiness he has never known.

Colleagues who knew Lewis as a hearty, good-humored drinking companion would probably take issue with Anthony Hopkins's stern portrayal. And those who know him through his books may sense a misrepresentation of how he viewed pleasure. Lewis indeed saw this life as a staging ground for the next, but he believed the "drippings of grace" on this planet are enough to awaken in us a thirst for eternal pleasures. He titled his autobiography *Surprised by Joy*, after all, and had the tempter Screwtape admit that pleasure "is His invention, not ours." For Lewis, sweet longings in this life were intimations of a redeemed creation to come, "the scent of a flower we have not found, the echo of a tune we have not heard, news from a country we have never yet visited."[1]

In the same lecture in *Shadowlands,* Lewis delivers his philosophy of pain, which becomes the movie's haunting motif. "Pain is God's megaphone to rouse a deaf world," he says confidently. The blows of the Sculptor, which hurt so much as they fall, are necessary to perfect our character. Lewis's confidence, though, weakens as he sees up close the devastating effect of the Sculptor's blows on the woman he loves.

The metaphor of pain as a megaphone is apt. One uses a megaphone to speak to a large crowd at long distance. As Lewis explains in *The Problem of Pain*, we might otherwise be tempted to assume this world is all there is. Pain reminds us that we live on a fallen planet in need of reconstruction. It keeps us from viewing this earth as a final Home.

Pain is a megaphone, though, not a headphone. For me, the Sculptor image in the film (I do not recall it in Lewis's writings) raises questions by portraying God too tidily as the direct agent of common human suffering. In the Gospels I have yet to find Jesus saying to the afflicted, "The reason you suffer from a hemorrhage (or paralysis or leprosy) is that the Father is working on you to build character." Jesus did not lecture such people; he healed them.

You need only read *The Problem of Pain* and *A Grief Observed* back-to-back to sense that Lewis's approach to this issue underwent change, a change that his letters also bear out. Pain became

for him less an intellectual puzzle and more a cry of anguish. I wish
Lewis had lived long enough to write a third book on pain, inte-
grating abstract speculation with personal experience. I have a
hunch his emphasis might have shifted from God as the Cause of
our suffering to God as the One who can redeem even the evil that
suffering may represent. He had seen that pattern of redeemed suffering in himself, in Joy Gresham, and in his Savior.

Shadowlands rightly sees pain and pleasure as two significant
themes for C. S. Lewis. Yet, apart from redemption, these themes seem
at times more a threat to his faith than its cornerstone. Understand-
ably. How can the moviegoing world understand redeemed pleasure
and redeemed pain if it does not believe in a Redeemer?

The movie ends with Lewis's faith intact, but shaky. In real life,
he emerged with an enriched hope for the ultimate transformation
of both pleasure and pain. He memorialized Joy Gresham in this
poem, now carved on her tomb:

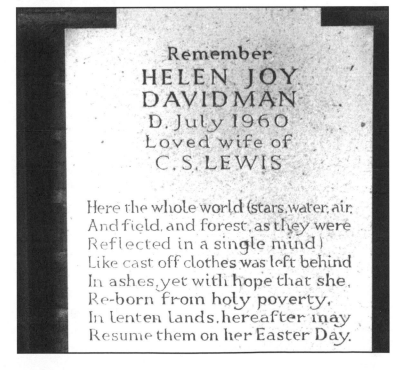

Remember
HELEN JOY
DAVIDMAN
D. July 1960
Loved wife of
C. S. LEWIS

Here the whole world (stars, water, air,
And field, and forest, as they were
Reflected in a single mind)
Like cast off clothes was left behind
In ashes, yet with hope that she,
Re-born from holy poverty,
In lenten lands, hereafter may
Resume them on her Easter Day.

ENCOUNTER IN A TWO-BIT PUB

Daniel Morris

Nancy-Lou Patterson, founder of the Department of Fine Arts and Distinguished Professor Emerita at the University of Waterloo, has since 1975 been the Reviews Editor of Mythlore, *the journal devoted to scholarly articles on mythopoeic literature in the United States. She passed along the following account to Stephen Schofield and* The Canadian C. S. Lewis Journal *in 1986. It was written by Daniel Morris, longtime family friend and godfather to the Patterson's daughter Francesca. "The first person I met who knew C. S. Lewis was Dr. Daniel Luzon Morris, who for many years was chemistry master at the Lakeside School in Seattle, Washington, where for four years (1958–1962) my husband was history master. Recently Dr. Morris sent me a sequence from letters he wrote in 1959 after a visit to Lewis in Cambridge. He has given me permission to send it to your Journal; and I think readers will enjoy it as much as I did."*

I called up Lewis (from London) at 3:00 this afternoon and arranged to meet him in Cambridge at 6:00. Got to Cambridge a little before 5:00, and wandered around the colleges, and ended up at King's College Chapel in the middle of Evensong. I wish I had known it would be going on. I had time to listen for only five minutes!—and it was wonderful. The clear voices of the choir, unhurried and unforced, picked up and carried lovingly by the vaults of the building.

Got to Magdalene College at 6:00. The porter directed me to Lewis's rooms: up a flight of rickety wooden stairs, along a rickety hall, to a door with Professor Lewis painted over it. The door was open, as was the next one inside. I knocked loudly. No answer. Went in and knocked at the inside one, which opened into a cold living room—but obviously lived in, because there was a telephone on the window seat, and an academic gown thrown over the back of an uncomfortable-looking sofa. Knocked a few more times, then retreated to the outer door. While I waited I had a chance to look at the floor, which is cheap, ancient pine boards frequently taken up and nailed down again—looks a little like a stable floor. A piece of ancient linoleum covered half the distance from the living room door to the outer door.

Finally, at 6:05 or so, an inner door opened, and Lewis appeared, looking so exactly like pictures of him that it was a bit startling. Red-faced, rather a fat face, could be called coarse, until it came into action. Medium height. Stoutish. He welcomed me and immediately asked if I was a teetotaller. I said no; and he said, Good, let's go to a pub across the street—that should moisten the conversation.

We went out and tried unsuccessfully to cross the street. It was jammed with cars and bicycles, moving just a trifle too fast to scurry between, but not fast enough to get clear. Glorious jam. Half the cyclists wore academic gowns (both boys and girls)—very skimpy ones, just enough to have a touch of black or dark blue. So Lewis and I wandered down toward the center of the town. Magdalene is the farthest north of the colleges; just across the Cam River from the rest of the town. As we walked, he said, "I'm the world's unluckiest man. Lived for years at Magdalen College, at the worst corner in Oxford, then had to come here where I can't even cross the street." He pronounced it "Maudlin." I said I was glad he had, because then I gathered that his present college was *Mag*dalene? No. Both are Maudlin. But half the people in

Cambridge think Oxford pronounces hers Magdalene, and half the Oxfordites think the same of Cambridge. Maudlin is the proper ancient pronunciation. The G was equivalent to the German final G as in Tag (which Germans pronounce Takh). So it was Makhd'lin. And Maud is the same name, which I didn't know.

By now we were at the pub—just an ordinary two-bit pub, none of the romantic olde inne stuff. He got himself a pint of bitter and me a glass of sherry (*wish* I liked beer, the proper drink for an occasion like that.) Then he asked me what I particularly wanted to see him about. I said, Nothing—I just wanted a chance to talk with him.

He said, "Oh; no agenda. Fine." He made me sit on his left, next to his good ear (easy to remember—that's my good ear too.) (But we were close enough together so my bad ear was no problem.) And then we just jawed for an hour and a quarter. From here on I won't try to make it sequential, but I'll try to get in the high points that I remember.

I forget how it came up, but he said something about his wife. I was surprised, and said so. I thought he was a bachelor. He was, until a year and a half ago. The lady was very ill, in fact wasn't expected to recover; and they married. She had cancer of the bones. X-rays showed that the bones were steadily deteriorating. He got "a good man"—he used those words—(I forget if he mentioned his name) who came in and laid his hands on her, with prayers. She got well. As far as he's concerned, there's nothing to call it but miraculous. The x-rays show it is now on the up-and-up. But whether you call it a miracle or not is a question. Do you call it a miracle when the doctors say somebody is going to get well, and they die?—a point I hadn't considered.

(Note, 1965—the account of the healing of his wife appeared in *The Atlantic* for January or February 1960, I believe. There he just calls her "a friend." Also I have discussed the matter with a doctor, who says that bone cancer *never* regresses spontaneously.)[1]

I mentioned Carol's[2] miraculous history, or a bit of it. And then he brought up the fact that his wife is . . . (Jewish), "Christian, of course." I didn't ask why "of course." But he says she has thrown a lot of light on the Old Testament for him. In fact the whole Bible. She comments on the fact that there are lots of places in the Bible, where, if we weren't so used to regarding it as sacred Scripture, we'd find it beautifully funny. She says there are lots of places where no Jew of intelligence could possibly have read it with a straight face, e.g. the spot where Abraham . . . (haggles with) the Lord on the number of good people there need to be in Sodom and Gomorrha, which has always tickled me. And he's sure that the parable of the Syrophoenician woman makes no sense unless you assume that there was a twinkle in Our Lord's eye from the very start of the conversation. His *denial* of healing to a supplicant is unthinkable considering everything else we know of him; and even more unthinkable that he should have given his help in response to a wisecrack from her. But if the whole thing was a playful interchange, on both sides, it makes good sense. (He elaborated on this, telling the story as it must have occurred.)[3] Likewise the parable of the unjust steward he interprets in that light—as a somewhat sardonic story. Incidentally, he thinks the master of the steward is the World—the Worldly world—and that the steward was being encouraged to "spoil the Egyptians." I'll have to read that one over again; it's one of the parables that solemn explainers make a mess of.[4]

He mentioned at one point that he was from the north of Ireland—that was when I said how much I enjoyed the Cockneys in East Ham—and he said he didn't see where the Irish got their reputation for wit. You heard ten times better wit any day on the streets of London than you did anywhere in Ireland. The Irish said things that the English sometimes thought were quaint, or funny, but they weren't being witty.

I brought up my ideas on machines, hoping they would strike a spark. They did. I was saying that I thought that machines were far too badly treated by philosophers; I thought they were wonderful. And he proceeded to blow off about 'em. At one point he said that he hates machines, and they hate him. Which gave me a chance to use my favorite quotation (from myself): "They adore me!" He looked sourly at me, and said he didn't know what that made me. We got talking about cars; and then widened the cars since the road would take 'em. Roads went on getting wider and wider, and so did cars. Finally this whole island would be just one road, with one car sitting on it. And we'd have to use little cars to get from place to place inside the big car.

Each of us had another drink. He another *pint* (not another glass) of bitter ale. Might explain his pudgy build. And when I brought it back to him from the bar I said, "It goes without saying, but I still want to say it: how very much I've enjoyed your books." He said, "We always love to hear it. Thank you." With a low bow.

Then he asked me what I was doing in England. Thence to mathematics, biochemistry, and the fourth dimension. He was much interested in the latter, and wanted to know if I knew of Hinton's ideas, including the one that with enough practice you can actually visualize the fourth dimension. I said that with all my practice, I can work with the figures easily enough, but not visualize them—it can't be done. He was insisting that the whole idea is pure imagination (he's read Hinton and Dunne and Ouspenski and Abbot) like the square root of minus one. And I wasn't willing to make it that imaginary, considering curvature of space, for example, which seems to be experimentally true—and meaningless, unless the universe really is four dimensional. He went into Dunne a good bit (that is, J. W. Dunne: *An Experiment in Time*, published in 1925) and he doesn't see (neither do I) why Dunne had to postulate an infinity of times at right angles to one another. Two times would cover the whole thing. Granted, that leaves a mystery as to what makes the thing run, but Dunne simply puts that off at infinity.

And thence to prevision, and extrasensory perception, and pre-destination. I mentioned (—a specific case, irrelevant here), which he agreed was a beautiful example of clairvoyance. And he came back with one of a friend of his. She dreamed that a pair of her friends were driving in a car and found themselves behind a truck-and-trailer on which was a big tree. They pulled out to pass, and at just that point the axle on the trailer broke. The tree fell off, on them, and killed them. The dream impressed her enough so she wrote the account of it and mailed it to the people concerned. (Thus documentary evidence before the fact exists.) Three weeks or so later they were driving in their car and found themselves behind a truck-and-trailer with a big tree on it. The husband was driving, and pulled out to start to pass, and his wife, more or less jokingly, said, "Be careful, you know what's supposed to happen!" So he swung back instead of passing—and it happened. The axle broke. The tree toppled. But they weren't under it.

Just as a tale, that's quite a tale! But we went on to bat it around from the point of view of prevision and predestination. There was a prevision of a future that didn't happen, but should have.

We scrapped quite a bit about the difference between the mind of the mystic and that of the genius in other fields. It came up in the middle of that discussion about the fourth dimension and the square root of minus one. He had pointed out that these are just plain inconceivable. And I said (or he said, as a response to something earlier of mine) "So is a triune God." He agreed there. And I said that statements like "God is triune" and "God is love" are essentially hypotheses, made by people who are going beyond the facts they know; but hypotheses in the light of which the known facts make sense. He came back with: "Ah, but those two statements about God are totally different in their nature. 'God is triune' is a theological statement; 'God is love' is one which can be made by a mystic who has had direct experience of it. The first is like a scientific hypothesis: it is based on a careful study of evidence, and of documents. The idea of God as love comes from the mystic who has actually tasted it." He used the word *gustatory* several times in this connection.

Then Lewis went back to a statement of his (that I quoted to him from a letter of his to me ten years ago) that a man may be perfectly sure that his wife is faithful, and a detective may be equally sure she is faithful. But the reasons for their belief are totally different in kind. The detective gets his from careful study of hotel registers and such, builds it up bit by bit. He kept insisting on this detective-vs.-husband difference.

Talking about machines, and thence to H-bombs, he said that he can't get bothered about the millions of people who will be killed in an H-bomb war—because it isn't the *number* of people killed or injured that matters. Whether it's thirty thousand or thirty million, each person dies only once, and his loved ones have the same feeling about his loss. *Quantity* of evil is no measure of anything.

In the course of our talk about Dunne, and such, he said it was a shame we couldn't control the rate of flow of time. As it was, the clock was rapidly moving on towards half-past seven, and the end of this delightful talk he was having with me.

And I (as usual pursuing the main point and losing the delightful side-turns) said, "Oh, no. I'd hate to have the time slow up or turn back. The most delightful time for me is always the present, not the past."

And he gently chided me for not in *any* way returning his pretty compliment—for not even recognizing it as it passed.

And I admitted I never do: never toss the ball back properly.

Magdalene College, Cambridge. Lewis's rooms on second floor, far left.

FORGETFUL RUDENESS

Hugh Sinclair

Hugh Sinclair was a contemporary of Lewis's at Magdalen College, Oxford. This piece originally appeared in The Guardian *on August 14, 1990, later reappearing in* The Canadian C. S. Lewis Journal. *Some of the journal's reading constituency felt the article was rude and demeaning to Lewis. However, Lewis's anathema for faculty administrative matters was well known, as was his occasional absent-mindedness. Instead of being upset, he probably felt relieved when he did not serve as vice president of Magdalen College's faculty a second year. Quitting this post appears to have been of his own doing, for according to his Magdalen College colleague A. J. P. Taylor, Lewis "never liked college administration. He became vice president, which is a two-year office, and after one year he said he couldn't do it any more.... [He] resigned as vice president after serving a single year."*

Personal recollections are colored by the teller's perspective, and no doubt Lewis is not as bad as some anecdotes would lead one to believe nor as wonderful as some stories euphemistically paint him. The following piece should be read, as best as humanly possible, from each participant's viewpoint. If you or I had been promised— in writing—a dinner conference at a specific time and date, then traveled many miles to be there, we would have every right to expect that promise to be fulfilled, as the hungry Patriarch of Pakrov certainly did. Likewise, if a speech by a well-known academic had been advertised to take place at a specific time and date, those who took time from their schedules to attend would be reasonably displeased if the speaker never materialized. On the other hand, humans make mistakes. Sometimes it is a miscommunication about dates or times. Sometimes the decision to accept or decline an engagement is misunderstood by one of the parties involved. Sometimes honest forgetfulness contributes to human error. Whatever the mitigating circumstances, no doubt Lewis—like the rest of us—was sometimes wrong. Some cases are salvageable, as when Lewis acted upon professor McFarlane's suggestion and took the Patriarch of Pakrov to dinner himself at the Eastgate Hotel. Others, like the London speech, cannot be remedied (probably because Lewis did not have a speech prepared, but also because he already had other plans for the day). The following account demonstrates some of Lewis's peccadillos, and if the reader is willing to look for it, there is even some humor detectable in Sinclair's account of Lewis trying to extract himself from these muddles.

C. S. Lewis was the only vice president of Magdalen within living memory not to be invited to undertake a second year of office, his first having been so disastrous. It is a function of the vice president to allot rooms for meeting or private entertainment. Lewis carried a little diary in which he sometimes entered the arrangements, more often not. Consequently two societies might find themselves holding lectures simultaneously. The efficient kitchen staff usually sorted out conflicting dinners.

One day I was breakfasting in the SCR Common Room, when at about 8:20 A.M. the chapel contingent entered: Benecke (great-grandson of Mendelssohn, who taught Classics and collected ornamental pigs), Adam Fox (the poetic Dean of Divinity), and Lewis; they sat at a central table to talk. In those days the *Times* carried on its center pages a list of the great events of the day, and I noted that Lewis was to give an important lecture in central

London at 10 A.M. I called across to ask him what train he was catching.

"Train? I'm not catching a train." I read the advertisement. "Oh, I seem to remember something about that. Well, I will not be there." Benecke carried the railway timetable in his head, although he never seemed to travel. He suggested a train that would shortly leave, and Adam Fox offered to get a taxi. But Lewis was adamant and resumed his bacon and eggs.

I telephoned in the afternoon and, as I expected, an enormous crowd assembled, waited, and slowly melted away; the organisers telephoned his house but got no reply; Warnie, expecting his brother to be in London, was out, and Lewis did not customarily answer the phone. Nor had he attempted to telephone that he would be absent.

On another occasion we had just left Hall after dinner and reached the SCR Smoking Room, then the Old Bursary, for coffee, when a knock on the door revealed an immensely impressive high official in the Eastern Orthodox Church, tall, clad in an embroidered black robe over which his white beard flowed, massive jewelled rings, gold chain with jewelled cross, and ebony walking stick with carved ivory handle. He asked for Lewis who somewhat reluctantly identified himself and, himself having a cup of coffee, courteously offered one to the visitor. He introduced himself as the Patriarch of Pakrov.

"I've come for my dinner," he firmly stated. "I'm afraid we've had dinner," Lewis replied. "You invited me to dine in your Hall and I want my dinner"; there was no doubt the Patriarch meant business. "Well, we dine at 7:15 and it is now 8:15; will you have some coffee?" "You invited me to dine at 8:15, and I want my dinner." "There must be some mistake; we always dine at 7:15. Please have some coffee." "Here is your letter which clearly states 8:15"; and this could not be denied; the Patriarch was not a person to trifle with.

"Oh, I'm afraid a mistake was made," Lewis lamely replied. "Your mistake does not affect the fact that I want my dinner." "I'm afraid the kitchen staff will have left. Please have some coffee." "I do not drink coffee. Your staff should be brought back." This, admirable in theory, was not easy in practice. "I am an old man who has travelled far for my dinner with you."

The Patriarch pointed out that he had been invited to dine and then to discuss the Synoptic Problem. This gave Lewis a possible line of escape. "Yes, I remember well. I am sure you disagree as I do with the interpretation by Lord Charnwood of the Gospels of Matthew, Mark and Luke, so just take a cup of coffee and sit in those armchairs to discuss the Synoptic Problem." "I am not interested in your charred wood and do not want to discuss the problem on an empty stomach. I have already pointed out that I have come for dinner and do not like coffee."

At this point Bruce Macfarlane, history tutor, broke the deadlock: "Lewis, the Eastgate Hotel across the road is still open for dinner." So thither Lewis and the hungry Patriarch went for what cannot have been a convivial meal, and no doubt the Synoptic Problem was not solved.

"HE SHOULD HAVE BEEN A PARSON"

Fred W. Paxford

OBSERVATIONS OF A GARDENER

For more than three decades, Fred W. Paxford was the caretaker at the Kilns, the place where the Moores, C. S. Lewis, and his brother Warren lived. Paxford and the others of the household were very fond of Lewis, as was he of them. The character of Puddleglum the Marshwiggle in The Silver Chair *is said to have been fondly modeled after Paxford, a character who outwardly appears pessimistic but inwardly is kindhearted and cheerful. Clyde Kilby, founder and original curator of the Wade Collection at Wheaton College, Illinois, once met Lewis and corresponded with him for a number of years. After Lewis's death, Kilby continued making trips to England, stopping by at times to visit Lewis's brother Warren and the working members of the Kilns. He wrote, "On my various visits to the Kilns I was often with Len and Molly Miller and Paxford, who was Lewis's gardener for thirty-four years. They all liked to talk about Lewis. Finally I proposed to Paxford that I would provide him with a notebook and he could jot down from time to time his memories. In due course he wrote fifty-three pages of notes. So here they are. Actually, I found them quite exciting." Lewis was a vivid "scene painter," whether he was writing letters, novels, or science fiction, and*

Paxford's descriptions of Lewis's love for nature and homely comfort shed light on the surroundings of the creator of Narnia. After Lewis's funeral in November 1963, it was a tearful Paxford who put his arm around Lewis's stepson Douglas Gresham and consoled him, "Ah, yer jus' gotter carry on, son. Yer jus' gotter carry on." Perhaps Paxford's highest compliment to Lewis came after the funeral with the reading of Lewis's will, in which he left Paxford a mere £100. Paxford, knowing Lewis was unskilled in many areas, such as mathematics, manual dexterity, athletics, or financial economics, accepted the small sum with the resigned comment, "Werl, it won't take me far, wull it?" He then added, "Mr. Jack, 'e never 'ad no idea of money. 'is mind was always set on 'igher things."

He titled these notes "Thirty-four years with Prof C. S. Lewis known at the Kilns as Mr. Jack."

When I became employed he had not long moved to the Kilns. It was damp and had a leaky roof on which we plastered tins of Righto, a pitch-like substance which was put on lots of perished tiles. The house stood in a little over nine acres of which about five were woodland in which were a few oaks and beeches, but mostly silver birch and conifers which seemed to attract a large quantity of birds of a lot of different species and nearly all the woodland animals, including badgers, foxes, and at one time lots of rabbits, in which Lewis was very interested. He remarked to me that the countryside was not the same when you didn't see the bobbing white tails of the rabbits. And I have seen him standing a long time watching the birds. And for years he would go for a walk in the wood most days, sometimes taking a scythe, and chop down brambles and nettles. He loved trees and would not have a tree cut down or lopped. When we wanted a few poles to make a bit of rose trellis, we had to get them when he was away for a few days, and cover the cuts with mud so they would not be seen. And when the trees were cut down opposite Magdalen College he was very cross.

The road to the Kilns was a very narrow lane with high hedgerows on each side and a very rough surface. There were only ten houses at the top of the lane, including two farms. There were no mains, gas, electricity, water or sewers, like the Kilns. Most of the houses had septic tanks and their own water supply. Some had candles and oil lamps. But the Kilns had its own water supply and a fifty-volt electric light plant. The water supply to the Kilns came from a spring at the top of the wood. The spring had a queer name with the locals. It was called the old mawle. And according to the locals the water was very good for bathing the eyes. They say that years ago people used to come for miles to fetch the water. I have often wondered if there is anything in this claim as I am over seventy and can still read a paper without glasses; and anyone who thinks that all water is the same should try drinking a glass of this water and compare it with a glass from the mains supply on a very hot day in the summer. I think they would, like me, change their tune. This spring was the water supply for the Kilns and three other houses for the sum of £2–0–0 a year.

The lake was the last clay hole that was dug before brickmaking ceased at the kilns nearby. It was roughly one hundred yards long and forty yards wide and ten feet deep, and a good water supply for the wildlife in the woods, and a popular drinking place for birds. It has pleasant memories for me as I saw things I would never have seen. One was thousands of tiny frogs, all over the drive and ground around the lake. You could not move without stepping on them. And I saw the only kingfisher I have ever seen. And going up there one day in the summer, a heron was standing on one leg. He must have been asleep as I got within a yard of him. He was a fairly regular visitor to the lake. I have seen him drop in lots of times. There were quite a lot of snakes in the woods. And at the shallow end of the lake there was an old willow tree leaning nearly flat into the water. One evening when the sun was still hot I happened to look at the tree, and the trunk was covered with snakes; there must have been fifty at least. I happened to step on a twig and they slithered into the water and dispersed. The lake was well stocked with fish, overstocked in fact, as when I fed the swans with bread each morning they would come around like a shoal of herrings and even jump up on the stone step that the bread was put on from which I have picked up fish of two or three pounds and put them back into the water.

The swans were a pair given to Mr. Lewis by the Provost of Worcester College. The cob was a spiteful old fellow when they had eggs, which they hatched out on two or three occasions, but they hardly ever reared more than one or two. As it was one of my jobs to feed the swans I always had to watch the cob in the breeding season as on more than one occasion he came up behind me when I had turned away and grabbed my trousers and often a bit of flesh, and flapped his wings a bit. But he was all right if I kept my eye on him. We had a young lady come to stay at the Kilns who offered to feed the swans. When I warned her about the cob, she said, "We are not afraid of swans, geese, or turkeys in Ireland." She picked up the basin of bread and went up to feed them. The next thing I saw was a white and frightened lady running down the path as hard as she could run. She simply threw down the basin and ran. The cob and his mate were helping themselves. I think Mr. Lewis had a soft spot for the swans as he would often take them the small tin of grain which they had every evening. We lost them both during the hard winters when the lake was frozen over. First the pen was killed by either a fox or a dog after a great battle as the rushes and brambles were squashed down over a wide area with feathers all over the place. The cob survived a few more years but was killed during another freeze-up. He too put up a great fight as again the rushes and brambles were squashed over a wide area, and feathers all over the place.

Some locals told me a man was drowned in the lake. It was one hot day in the summer and the brickmakers wagered among themselves who would undress and be up to the lake and into the water first. One man dived in and the rest did not miss him for a few minutes. They found he had dived in and got stuck in the mud. Whoever won the bet—I expect the money would have been spent on beer. The brickmakers were very fond of it. They used to send the sandboy down to the pub (of which there were three about 50 yards apart) for a jar of beer. He always had half a pint of beer, which was called a sandier for years after brickmaking stopped.

The fish in the lake suffered badly during two dry summers; each time it killed off thousands. On the first occasion I had to take the boat and rake out all the large ones and bury them as the lake was used for bathing and of course in the hot weather they soon began to smell. The Kilns, as the name suggests, was a brickworks and the kilns and the drying shed we converted into stores for coke and coal and a laundry. The drying shed was a large barn which was very handy for a wood store and we had a large quantity of wood until the war came, when we had to saw most of it up to burn. C. S. Lewis and his brother helped to do a lot of the sawing.

At the Kilns was a good hard tennis court which C. S. Lewis always said was a blot on the horizon. When I first came the household consisted of Mrs. Moore, her daughter Maureen, C. S. Lewis (referred to as Mr. Jack), and two maids. Mrs. Moore was a daughter of the Dean of Kilmour, who used to visit once or twice a year. We had several Irish maids, and they all described him as a great guy. Mrs. Moore used to run the house and do quite a bit of cooking.

She was very fond of animals and kept a few, poultry which she loved to fuss with. But Mr. Jack always said that the best place for a chicken was on the table. At least we always had plenty of fresh eggs. She also had two dogs and two cats, always well fed. She was a great lady, very fond of Ireland and the Irish and of mothering people. If any of the household was a little off color, out came the thermometer. She was like a mother to Mr. Jack, and he always called her Mintoes. She was also very good to me. She had one funny little habit when she was bottling fruit and shaking it down in the bottles: she always had part of her tongue showing between her lips. She was also very fond of flowers, never had too many. She bottled a lot of fruit and gave a lot of it away. She gave a lot of eggs away as well. She had a kind nature. Anyone who came to the Kilns for help nearly always went away with money, and if it was a man, a handful of cigarettes.

As I have said, Mr. Jack was fond of animals. He always told me how he liked to go and see the deer at the College. He also seemed to like the badger and would talk about brock for a long time. Needless to say he disliked blood sports and never seemed to have any interest in any sports or games, though I think he liked to play chess. He seemed to avoid tennis parties at the Kilns. And he never had any interest in cars, only as a means of getting from here to there; and even then he much preferred to travel by train. Some of his tastes in food were queer. He said he would much rather have a pigeon roasted or in a pie than a pheasant; he said they were very dry. He liked potatoes baked in their own skins in the oven, and unlike most Irish people he didn't have the idea that Irish potatoes were the best in the world. Clothes never seemed to worry him until the last few years of his life. He always seemed quite happy in an old pair of corduroys or flannels and an old sports jacket. He would not bother about shoes unless a sprig came through the sole or his foot got wet; then he would find a big hole in the sole. Although he wrote a lot of children's books, I don't think he was all that fond of them; but I may be wrong. He would often say, "Spare the slipper and spoil the child." He seemed to think it applied to the present generation. Mr. Jack and his brother, both fond of walking, took quite long walks most afternoons. And they often went on walks during the holidays. On one holiday I remember taking them a few miles out of Oxford and coming to the bottom of a steep hill which looked at least a mile long. Mr. Jack said, "Stop here, we will start walking." I said, "Why not go to the top of the hill in the car?" He wouldn't hear of it, and they both got out. He often said nothing was nicer than a long walk and then a stop at a pub and have a nice crust of bread and cheese and a pint of best bitter. He often spoke of the lovely crusty cottage loaf, and said the modern soggy loaf couldn't compare with it. He had a good word for English cheddar cheese. I think he liked most cheese. He once told me that Gloucester Green was never as good as when modern cowsheds came on the scene.

He was very fond of jokes. Country jokes seemed to amuse him most. Once we were coming up Kiln Lane during an election and there was a conservative placard hung out by one of the houses. He said he would have to do his duty that afternoon and vote for the member; and I said I should have to go down in the evening and cancel his vote. It quite amused him. On another occasion I had to fetch him from College one morning between midnight and one o'clock. He had wined and dined fairly well, and a black cat crossed the road in front of the car. I said how lucky for a black cat to cross our path early in the morning. He said, "I didn't see a cat. What pub have you been to? They must have good beer." I had not been to a pub at all and he knew it.

I must write some of the country jokes he liked. In most English villages years ago they used to form their own clubs and once a year they used to have a get-together and a day off work, and a good meal and a booze-up. The local brass band marched round the village and sometimes played at a few large houses in the village. Usually a big man carried a flag to lead the band. The man in my village was six feet tall and hard as nails. But it wanted a strong man as the flag pole was twenty feet long and quite heavy. Of course the band had drinks at the large houses where they played; and there was a pleasure-fair: roundabouts and swing boats, etc. The band played at the fair as well. This all started at ten in the morning, and they all marched back to the large barn where the meal was laid on. Meat was given by local farmers. And after the meal plenty of drink and another march around the village about four o'clock for all those who could still walk or march. And then back to the barn about seven for more food and drink. All the club members carried blue staves with yellow tops which were very handy to help them home at the end of the day—those that could get home. There was only one fly in the ointment: it used to finish up with a few free fights. The club days were called feasts in some villages. In my story a man whose club day was on the Monday went to the next village on the Saturday evening to have a drink with a friend. When they sat down with their drinks he turned and said, "Bist 'a cumming up to our feast on Monday? We got two sorts of bacon—mutton and buff." As most people kept a pig in those days, on club day—just as the band was marching by—a pig got out of its sty and put its two front feet on the garden wall. And of course after that it was: "Oh, that's the place where they put the pig on the wall to see the band go by."

Lots of village cricket matches were only an excuse for a booze-up. They often had a barrel of beer on the field. During one game the fast bowler dismissed the other village team for a fairly low score. As he was not much of a bat and was the last man in, he had a few good sips of beer. But his team didn't get many runs, and with only him to bat, they still wanted three or four runs to win. So the captain, seeing the state he was in, went up to him and said, "Look, Bill, when you get out there you will see three balls coming. Hit the middle one. Then we can win." Bill went to the wicket, took guard and faced up to the first ball, which he missed, and down went his stumps. When he went back the captain asked him if he saw the three balls coming? Bill said, "Yes." "Well," the captain said, "I told you to hit at the middle one." Bill said, "Ah, I did that. But thee didn't tell me which bat to use."

Another story Mr. Jack always seemed to like was about a landlord who ran a pub. He was a man who always had something better than other people. One evening the customers in the bar were talking about the quality of their binoculars. The landlord said he had a pair that if you went outside on a Sunday night and looked at a church that was three miles away, his binoculars would bring the church so near that you could hear the congregation singing.

Another joke Mr. Jack liked to hear was about a country woman who hated to wear new shoes. She said she had to wear them for a month before she could get them on.

I have written these few jokes to emphasize that although Mr. Jack often looked rather sad he did enjoy a joke and a good laugh.

It was a pity Mr. Jack could not have lived a few more years until the moon landing. He was very interested in the stars and moon and liked a trip to the observatory. How thrilled Mr. Jack would have been if he could have seen the rock and dust brought back from the moon! He would have been pleased to know that the distance had been so well estimated by the mathematicians, as he always used to argue that they were accurate, when I used to doubt it. Funny: he used to like to have little arguments; and he never got angry in an argument. One thing we often argued about was coal. He said it was decomposed residue of vegetation, mostly giant frond. Though I am not as religious or good as I ought to be I like to think that the earth and everything it produces was made by God for the good of man: a very old-fashioned outlook now, I suppose. I wonder if by having little arguments with several people he either strengthened his own opinion or made a new one? Or if it was his way of trying to get at the truth?

Mr. Jack should have been a clergyman. He would have made a great parson. When he preached at Quarry Church, it was always packed. He had a full clear voice which could be heard all over the church; and he nearly always brought a bit of humor into the sermons; and people seemed to like this. On a few occasions I had to drive him in to Oxford to preach in St. Mary's. As he always liked to be early, I parked the car and went to the service, and the church was always packed.

Of course he was Irish, born in Belfast. But he liked England better than his own country. He liked to go to Ireland for a holiday. I asked him several times when he came back if he wouldn't like to go back to Ireland to live, and he always said no. He must have been one of the few people who like English weather. He always said it was much better than having several months of hot sunshine and the rest of the year rain every day. And he said our weather was often used as a way to start conversation which would otherwise not have started.

Coming back to Mrs. Moore and Mr. Jack, in the days before they came to Oxford, they lived in Bristol. And Mrs. Moore often told me that they were not very well off then. They lived in a house which had an orchard and garden. And she said that four of them lived on thirty shillings (£1–10–0) a week and a few shillings she got out of a few poultry, and by selling some of the fruit, which included cherries. She would often talk about the cherries. The four people must have been Mrs. Moore, her son and daughter, and Mr. Jack. Even in those days when things were much cheaper it must have been, as she often said, fairly hard times.

Once when they went to Ireland on holiday they went to a boarding house that was run by two sisters who, strangely enough, were named Moore. And when one sister passed on, Mr. Jack and Mrs. Moore brought the other one to the Kilns. And they bought a bungalow for her which I erected in the corner of the garden. It was fitted up with cosy stove, bath, and toilet, and electric light. She must have been a real Irish lady as she was very superstitious. Each New Year's Eve I used to sit up until midnight. And when the new year came in, I went up and had a glass of wine with her, as she said a fair-haired man must be the first to cross the threshold in the new year. She lived in the bungalow for five years. When she passed on I always admired Mr. Jack as when she was buried he was the only one to pay her the last respects and follow her to the grave.

The Kilns, Headington Quarry, Lewis's house, 1930–63

REMINISCENCES OF THE OXFORD LEWIS

James Houston

James Houston taught as a University Lecturer for twenty-three years at Oxford. In 1970 he became founding Principal of Regent College, then also its Chancellor, in Vancouver, British Columbia, Canada. He is still Professor of Spiritual Theology at Regent. When Stephen Schofield founded The Canadian C. S. Lewis Journal *in 1979, Dr. Houston wrote him, "It so happens that I knew Lewis because he was a member of a group that met on Saturday evenings in the apartment of Dr. Nicholas Zernov, with whom I lived before I was married, in the late 1940s and early 1950s. Lewis was a regular member of our group and we had interesting times together in dialogue, with men like Professor Mascal and Professor D'Antreves. The subjects ranged widely, and of course Lewis was in the middle of controversy and argument. He was of course very brilliant. But we never dreamt that he would have such wide recognition that he has. While I admire tremendously his brilliance and his communication of faith to the world, nevertheless, I cannot help but see this as a sad contrast to the lack of obedience and commitment by other scholars in the Christian faith. Perhaps he stands out simply as evidence of the lack of commitment that others might have to follow in his own ministry and gifts."*

The following remarks are an edited version of an informal talk presented to a special gathering of the Southern California C. S. Lewis Society in November 1982. Dr. Houston's talk was tape recorded, transcribed by George Musacchio, and edited from the transcription by Ken Matthews. This article then appeared in The LampPost, *volume 7, number 2, issued in August 1983. This has now been further edited for this publication by Dr. Houston, being reprinted here with permission.*

If you look to see who the people are who have said and written so much about Lewis—his friends, his interests, and his theology for that matter—nearly all are Americans.[1] This reveals more about American religious culture than it does about Lewis, of "Christian significance" in association with great "leaders," especially when Lewis seemed to give intellectual respectability to the Christian life. So this helps to explain why Lewis has been more popular in America than ever he was in England. The adulation of Lewis in America thus tends to give a distorted view of Lewis's own place among his peers at Oxford, and its own distinct cultural nuances. So the following reminiscences are given from within the Oxford setting shortly after the war, just to add for the record of Lewis's context.

Let's start with Lewis and his friends. If you read Chad Walsh or Clyde Kilby or later American admirers of Lewis, you get the impression that Lewis had a few close friends within the Inklings, and that was it. In fact, one book states that Lewis had no Christian friends in Oxford other than Tolkien—his colleague in Anglo-Saxon—and Hugo Dyson, another English faculty member. Yet now we know that Lewis was married secretly in a public registry office for nearly a year before these friends ever knew about it. Lewis's professional conviviality with many was not the same as intimacy with his brother—a boyhood friendship—and his bizarre marriage. Besides the Inklings, Lewis attended other regular meetings. I was part of the frequent Saturday evening meetings in 27 Norham Road, where Nicholas Zernov shared an apartment with me from 1947 to 1953. His wife, Melitza, was a dental surgeon practicing in London. After I married in 1953, the mutual convenience of living together changed for us all.

As Melitza has recorded, C. S. Lewis once called Nicholas Zernov "an institution in Oxford life." In his post as Lecturer in Eastern Orthodox culture (1943–1966) he was attached to both history and theology faculties, with the university as academic pioneer in Orthodox studies. He was a lay starets,[2] who had always wanted to be a monk. Instead, he was given the vision to share religious convictions within a scholarly milieu, something that inspired Lewis and other of Nicholas's friends in new ways. After a buffet supper in our apartment, other regular visitors—along with Lewis—would be Eric Mascal, Hugo Dyson, Austin Farrer, Gervase Mathew, Professor D'Antreves, Basil Mitchell, as well as three remarkable ladies: Mrs. Sutherland, Margerie Reeves, and Nadejda Gorodetsky. Occasionally Anthony Bloom, then rector of the Russian church in London, might be there, and there were even visits from the monks of Athos. It was a fascinating but strange world for me as the sole Evangelical in this admixture of Roman Catholics, Greek and Russian Orthodox believers, and Anglicans. Lewis was clearly recognized to be a leader in our conversations over papers read to the group, but he was only one of several, equally influential speakers.

I got to know Hugo Dyson through another colleague of mine in geography who was also professor at one stage in Dyson's own Reading University. When Dyson came to Oxford in 1945, I got to know him pretty quickly. If you think that Lewis was witty and loquacious and always said the last word, you should have seen Dyson. I think Dyson was the smarter of the two. It was amazing, this tour de force; the wittiness, the intense enthusiasm of the man—he was alive to life in a remarkable way, and yet very gentle, very loving. It was Dyson, if you remember, who went on that long walk with Lewis after dinner at the back of Magdalen and where, if one can date the event, Lewis's conversion probably took place.[3] Dyson was a remarkable man, the heart and soul of any dinner party and conversation. And of course, Lewis and Dyson together were really just tremendous.

Another strong personality, witty and sharp, was Professor D'Antreves, who held the chair in Italian studies. He was quite a character. D'Antreves was a committed believer, a Catholic who had written a significant, popular book on natural law for Home University Press. The paper D'Antreves contributed to our group on this subject fascinated Lewis, and he and D'Antreves debated with each other in a lively cut-and-thrust fashion.

Another person who does not now get the attention he deserves is Gervase Mathew, a Roman Catholic priest. He had a remarkable range of interests, from archaeology in East Africa to the Byzantine Studies in which he was a lecturer, and he had great understanding of the Coptic Church in Egypt. He also was usually a member of our Saturday night group.

Then there was Austin Farrer, the theologian, who later became the warden at Keble College, and who wrote on symbolism in Mark's Gospel. He and E. L. Mascal, who later became Professor of Moral Theology at King's College, London, were the two theologians in the group. Farrer was a very sensitive person, shy, very erudite. He'd been a Fellow and Chaplain of Trinity College when Lewis first knew him.

I have mentioned that we had a number of ladies in our group. Margerie Reeves, a medieval historian, was a Fellow of St. Anne's College. She did a remarkable piece of work with some of the Franciscan mystics, such as Angela Feligno, and others of that period. She was very active with the Student Christian Movement and was a devout Christian—was recognized as such by all in the University. She was very much a leader in our group; she was always there taking part in the planning of programs. She was also involved in a group of dons from other universities that met at Windsor Castle that she helped to organize; and she often invited Lewis to that group as well. Margerie was a first-class lady.

Then there was a Mrs. Sutherland, a Fellow of Lady Margaret Hall, whose specialty was Provençal studies. She did not take the stand of being a committed Christian, but she was very interested, and a beautiful person in her own character. She often came along to the group with her husband, a librarian in the Bodleian.

One of the shy members of the group was Nadejda Gorodetsky, whom my wife got to know better when we became neighbors in Bardwell Road. Her wonderful book, *The Humiliated Christ in Modern Russian Thought*, had been published in 1939, and she was to write other more sophisticated works of scholarship. But her own beautiful humility eclipsed her within the Zernov circle.

Then, of course, there was my friend Nicholas Zernov, who had just resigned as the first Secretary of the Fellowship of St. Alban and St. Sergius, to take up a lectureship in Oxford. He had founded the House of St. Gregory and St. Macrina to improve ties between Anglican and Orthodox communities and was very active trying to help Anglicans in England understand Eastern Orthodoxy in Russia. Nicholas and I really had a most engaging time together. My friend Douglas Johnson, General Secretary of Inter-Varsity Fellowship, nicked-named us Exhibits A and B, because I came from a low-church Evangelical background that Nicholas had never encountered before, and Nicholas, of course, was Russian Orthodox. I was privileged to meet the monks from Athos from our domestic live-in arrangement and would say to my friends, "Have you ever met monks from Athos?" Well, they never had. So I would reply, "Now's your chance. Come and see us." Likewise, his white and gray Russian friends from Paris were very doubtful about my authenticity. I remember one occasion when his elder sister came over from Paris to see how her brother was behaving. She looked at me very doubtfully and said, "Oh, a Christian. But can you say the Apostle's Creed?" I replied that I could. "Well, say it." So I said it. "And do you really believe it?" This was still not a period when Lewis's popularity for *Mere Christianity* had become established. But deep as the religious divide between Nicholas and myself then seemed, I still carry the great impression he made upon me as he practiced his rich devotional life in the quietness of his room in vocal prayer that I heard daily.

I have to say this about myself. I didn't take advantage of these opportunities as I might have done for two reasons. First, I was dreadfully shy. I used to cross the road rather than say good morning to my own colleagues. I was often tongue-tied when I could have had the opportunity of really finding out much more about people. I really should have come to live in America for the first ten years of my postgraduate days; then I would have been released and had the ontological freedom that you have over here. And I think you'll agree that we're all very cosseted socially. To give you an example, I used to meet a Fellow from Balliol College at the same corner of the road as I commuted to my work. We were going in opposite directions. We must have passed each other around that same corner every morning for about fifteen years. Sometimes we looked, sometimes we didn't, but we never saluted each other. And then, in 1972, I saw him in the street in Vancouver. I ran across the road, almost embraced him, invited him for dinner that night, and he rolled with laughter (and I did too), because we had to wait until we'd crossed the seas into a different culture to speak to each other for the first time!

Such stiffness in British academic culture reinforced one's own innate shyness. I think we used to envy some of the Americans who came to see Lewis, because with a breeziness and a freedom, they would simply go straight up to him, without waiting on any introduction, and let him know who they were. It seemed as if that kind of social aggressiveness was not readily accepted in the culture. So I think that Lewis was really ministered to by American visitors and American correspondents. Their boldness was a breath of fresh air to his own shy soul. We always rather envied the Americans who could get away with it, and rather wished we could do the same. Of course, I did get rather tired sometimes of people who wrote to me, who were coming to Oxford and wanted me to arrange a dinner party or ask Lewis to invite them over for lunch. I remember doing this for Dr. Frank Gaebelein and other American visitors. It seemed as if their only memories of Oxford were of having been introduced to Lewis.

Our group was very informal. On any given Saturday we might be twenty to thirty in the group, including a number of visitors, senior students doing B. Litt.'s or doctorates that might join us. Lewis didn't always hold the floor. But he gave an occasional paper. I remember vividly a paper that he gave which critiqued Mariolatry. Of course, Gervase Mathew and D'Antreves and a number of others really jumped on him, and he loved that—he loved to be outnumbered. Lewis was thought by many, I think, especially by the philosophers in the university, to rather cheat at this debating game, because (although it came out better in his books) in actual dialogue with people, he was very fond of creating an incongruity in the illustrations and analogies that he drew. The sheer incongruity of the comparison or analogy would draw derisive laughter, and under that diversion, he would duck and dash off in another direction—almost like a magician's sleight of hand in the way he would make his analogies and then run away from the logical path he should have followed.

On one memorable occasion in 1948 at the Socratic Club (the Monday night debating society established at Oxford by Stella Aldwinkle, then Chaplain of University students at St. Aldates' Church) he had a formidable opponent in Miss G. E. M. Anscombe. She was a Catholic philosopher at Somerville College. That night, Lewis was beaten. And it was a turning point in Lewis' apologetic. He never quite came back to that kind of confrontation. Years later, this particular debate led him to rewrite chapter three of his book *Miracles*, "The Cardinal Difficulty of Naturalism."

My own personal relations with Lewis from these Saturday night meetings were limited. We used to meet as a group, but I do remember one conversation with Lewis about the Vanaukens.[4] Mrs. Vanauken was already a committed Christian, and she told me that her husband, Sheldon, had also become a Christian. On that Saturday night, I told Lewis: "You know this young American that you've been in touch with, who's doing his B. Litt. here? Your correspondence has been so faithfully blessed and now he's taken a stand." And he said, "Oh, I'm so glad." And then as if to say, "You're not getting to my soul that way!" he immediately switched the conversation on to something else. I was exasperated, because from my own Evangelical perspective, I wanted him to sort of work up on this, and to say more about it, but he would not. That showed me very vividly Lewis's intense shyness, especially in matters of faith. There really were two sides to Lewis. On the one hand, he was quite prepared—in apologetics—to be really up-front, and he did more than anyone else in England was doing at that time in his debates, in the broadcast talks, and in the books he was writing; but when it came to personal discussion with him, as to his own soul, as to the reality of religious experience in his own heart, he would not be drawn.[5]

I think the reason for this was his own cultural background, because in many ways he was a remarkable paradox. He was often dubbed a fundamentalist by his friends (although fundamentalist isn't the right word in England—Evangelical is their term—but an Evangelical draws the same dirty looks there as a fundamentalist tends to do here). Lewis was viewed as an Evangelical, but he had no cultural connections with Evangelicals. He had no friends among them. (As I say, I couldn't be considered a friend.) His friends were all Anglo-Catholic or Catholic. And yet, he set himself over against some elements of that culture, so that he was, as I say, a contradictory character. Of course, his own wit and debating skill were sharpened by the fact that he loved these friends yet in many respects held completely different views from them. In fundamentals, they were the same, but when it came to ecclesiology, they were very often quite sharply different, such as is evidenced by the aforementioned debate in our group over Mariolatry.

Lewis, of course, has been adopted by the Evangelicals in America in a way that would have made him very uncomfortable. He didn't associate with them; he didn't think of himself as one of them. I was then linked with the Evangelical Union, the Christian Union in Oxford, as a senior member, but although I tried to persuade the student committee to invite him to speak, they would not have him. This may seem remarkable today, when you think how students have been blessed by his books. I was also the chairman of the Graduate's Fellowship, and again, we never had Lewis, though we did have one or two other people who were considered somewhat suspect at the time.

But in that culture, we no more talked about religion to our colleagues than we would talk about our kidneys. It was the concealed part of one's being. We didn't live in a culture like our North American culture, where one can unashamedly talk about religion. I suppose one of the reasons for the difference has to do with church attendance.

Then, in the fifties, church attendance was only about 5 or 6 percent. It wasn't a popular thing to go to church. The chapels were becoming the laughing stock of many of the dons. There was a rumor in the fifties that we should start thinking about changing our chapels into libraries. This actually did take place in the late sixties in several cases. Those who attended chapel were just a miserable little minority. Lewis had little support from the chaplains at Oxford at that time. They were academic chaplains, who in a sense were there in spite of being chaplains. They were there basically because of their teaching posts and were usually liberal, and really snorted at Lewis. This "cheap religion" that he was popularizing was something to which they were not sympathetic.

Those of us who were Christians therefore stood out as Christians in our own common rooms. I can deeply understand why Lewis wrote *That Hideous Strength*, because he is describing his own Magdalen Common Room, and the struggles and the sneers that he got there from his smart colleagues; nothing could be more outrageous to them than that a man should not only talk religion, but should publish it, and be known and have a reputation way beyond theirs because of religion and not scholarship. Thus, his scholarship tended to be overlooked by many in the 1950s, because he was too popular as a religious writer.

I can't go into the details of how he must have suffered, but I can tell you how I suffered on two occasions to illustrate the kind of sensitivity that we faced in the college at that time for having any religious stance. On one occasion I had spoken at the annual meeting of a local Scripture Union Meeting for young people. In those days the local *Oxford Mail* had all of our *curricula vitae* ready for our obituaries. A Christian journalist on the staff of the *Mail* took this opportunity of writing me up because I had taken this meeting on Sunday afternoon. On Monday night I went into the Common Room where Alan Bullock was then the master of St. Catherine's. He and his cronies were rolling with laughter at this write-up about Houston and his religious antics.

I never more wished the floor to swallow me up when I realized what they were reading, and how they were ridiculing the whole thing. The other occasion that branded my memory was when I was sitting at dinner with a visiting chaplain from another college who had just written a commentary on Daniel. I said, "Oh, I enjoyed reading your commentary," and he turned to his host and said, "I didn't know that you had another theologian in this college." To which the host replied, "We don't." "Well, who is this guy sitting beside me?" "Oh, he is our Geography Fellow." "Well, how come he's read my book and you haven't?" (This was because he had asked the host whether he had read the commentary.) "Oh, he's an Evangelical." And, of course, that was the end of the conversation.

Besides religion, another thing that was highly suspect was that you should in any way publicly trespass out of your own territory, your own academic pitch. I remember one occasion when Ayers, the Logical Positivist, was dining with us from New College. I was sitting with him, and I started to ask him one or two philosophical questions, and he turned to his host who was a fellow in philosophy in my college and said, "I didn't realize that you had another Fellow in philosophy here." The host replied, "We don't." That was the end of the conversation. He just refused to speak to me anymore. So there was a lot of arrogance that went with these kinds of attitudes. In contrast is the American free-flowing acceptance— not looking at you in terms of your academic role. This is health;

it is freedom. It is so different from the Oxford atmosphere in which Lewis lived and worked.

A. J. P. Taylor, the modern historian at Magdalen, was one of Lewis's implacable foes.[6] He, more than anyone else, really was bitter against Lewis's "religious antics," as he called them. And, of course, his antagonism threatened the club life of the college, because when you're dining together, day in and day out, week in and week out, you really have to have certain norms of acceptability. You can't stick out like a sore thumb. It's not like living at home and having no social relationships at work. You destroy the club when you stand out as Lewis did. Not that he was deliberately trying to do it, as you know.

Lewis's college, Magdalen, used to have three or four senior fellowships, which were open for a two- or three-year period. About five of them became vacant every year. Of course, scores of people applied, and when you've singled out, say, fifteen candidates for five positions, they're all brilliant, all obvious, suitable candidates. So how do you sort them out? Well, Magdalen didn't have the procedures of Gideon. This is a true story. What they did was to dine them, and for dessert serve them cherry pie; and if they swallowed their cherry pits in shyness, then of course, they were condemned because they were too obsequious. If they spat their cherry stones out in the plate, then they were obviously too vulgar. So the adroitness with which they moved the stones onto their forks and thence onto the plates was the test for acceptance. The story illustrates the kind of conventionality and acceptability that you had to have. And if they were upset about the way you ate cherry pie, you can imagine what they must have felt about somebody who had become so nationally recognized for his religious life.

In this atmosphere, the Socratic Club met on Monday nights. Stella Aldwinkle energetically got this going. She was a fond admirer of Lewis, bless her heart, and would have done all she could to have married him, I think. She was then attached to St. Aldate's, which was viewed as a sophisticated foreign mission, and Lewis, with a certain amount of goodwill, was brought in and became very active in it. The activities of the Socratic Club didn't help Lewis in his standing with his colleagues, because that was bringing right into the portals of the university this kind of apologetic for the Christian faith. Another thing that didn't help Lewis was that his training in philosophy was really post-First World War, that is to say, basically in Hegelianism, whereas the philosophy after the Second World War was Logical Positivism, which had come from the Vienna Circle through German refugees in the thirties into Oxford. The logical positivists were then freezing university life because nearly all the philosophy dons in the post-war era in Oxford were very much affected by this whole new way of looking at philosophical systems. In a sense, then, Lewis's debating style was really rather old fashioned.

The strength of Lewis's writing relates to a university system where in the humanities everyone had to write from seventy-five to over a hundred essays during their undergraduate training. You would have a tutorial each week on average. Some had two. Eight weeks of essays, eight essays per term, twenty-four per year. Multiply that by three. That's the minimum number of essays that you write. You brought your essay to your tutor; sometimes he would slouch and sometimes fall asleep. The story is told about one tutor (it wasn't Lewis) who shut his eyes and the student thought he really had gone off to sleep, so when he finished his essay and got no response, he read it again. Years later, when this alumnus introduced himself to his old teacher, the tutor said, "Oh yes, old Boggs, I remember you. You were the fool who read his essay twice, and once was bad enough." It was a system that was much abused in the sense that so much depended on your getting a smart tutor. A don had a choice of filling one of three roles. He could be a college man with various useful functions as an administrator; or he could be a researcher and get on with his writing; or he could be a good teacher. I don't think Lewis was a very good tutor. He didn't have enough patience to listen to students, and he sometimes confused the names of his students and he even confused their standings. I suppose this is a problem when you've got fifteen or twenty, and he was only supposed to do fifteen hours of tutorial a week, but I expect he did more than that on occasion. You had to cover the whole range of an honors school—you might swap a few special subjects, but at least two-thirds of the teaching you had to do yourself. So it was a system in which you were absorbed in essay writing and critiquing. Then there were private dinner parties like the Martlets that Lewis belonged to, in which a group of friends would meet together to take interest in a particular topic. And the basis of your getting together was to listen to one another's essays. The papers that we read to one another in our Saturday night group were the same kind of thing. The atmosphere was one of the litterateur, of the critic of essays. What really gave Lewis his skill, I think, was that he went out of his way far more than the rest of his colleagues to share his writings with his friends. One of the things that gives such quality to Lewis's work is that his statements were polished like diamonds with many facets, coming no doubt from a great deal of discussion, of arguing together.

The other aspect of Lewis's life—his shyness about his personal life—relates to the fact that many of the Oxford dons, Lewis included, were really awfully gauche in personal relationships, in relating prudently with other people. There were great barriers so that people couldn't readily intrude into their lives. If you weren't introduced, you weren't introduced—period—that was it. Yet on the other hand, many of the dons had been brought up in prep schools so that they really had not had much home life. They hadn't really known their mothers from the age of seven or eight. And their fathers were very distant figures. Lewis suffered all his life, I think, from having an absent or at least a distant father. The death of his mother sealed that for him as a child; and the prep school, the private school, or public school as we call it, intensifies unisexual relationships. There was not much relationship with girls. And to come up to Oxford was to intensify all that, because we were a male-dominated society.

There were only five women's colleges to the twenty-eight or twenty-nine men's colleges until the 1970s when we began to have them mixed; and to give you an example of the kind of attitudes that we had toward women: in 1968, a brash young Fellow who had spent too long in America put on the agenda of our college the possibility that we might become a mixed college. When this matter was read out, our medieval historian, with great dignity, said, "Well, gentlemen, if this is the matter for your discussion this afternoon, I shall have to go look after my garden. I have my roses to water." And off he stalked, and the thing was postponed from the agenda for another two years. We heard no more about it.

Even marriage was taboo in this atmosphere. When I got married in 1953, I was thought to have failed my profession. I had really dropped out of the league because obviously, if you're a married man, you're distracted. You cannot do your scholarship as you're expected to. This was a good sixty to seventy years after dons were released to marry. Until the 1880s, any don who married had to resign his post with the university. But it was still looked on with great disfavor three-quarters of a century later. We still had living with us the first child of an Oxford don who was married by permission of the College.

The dons really lived in another world. It was very much eighteenth century. I suspect that all these factors contributed in giving the dons a lot of naïveté about personal life, personal relationships. As bursar of our college, I lived between upstairs and downstairs, and would often hear the college scouts, who were usually shrewd and wise about human relations, laughing about things they had heard, the attitudes of some of the dons, or even the greediness of their table manners. The international reputation they might have for scholarship was no indication of their prudence in personal life.

I suspect that, with all that background, Lewis was himself a bit gauche about his personal life. Mrs. Moore, for example, put him in quite an extraordinary situation. I'm sure it was out of his sheer good nature that he took her into his home and allowed her to tyrannize his whole life as she did for so many years.[7] And even the almost offhand way in which he married Joy Davidman so that she would be able to remain an immigrant in Britain was a remarkable thing for a long-term bachelor to do. But I think that all of this is explained to some extent by the social attitudes and the protections I have mentioned, that existed in a very unreal world.

Wingfield Morris Hospital. Here Lewis married Joy Davidman.

SIGHTINGS

Burton K. Janes

BILLY GRAHAM

*Few of the people who met C. S. Lewis achieved any large measure of
fame themselves. Some such as John Betjeman, Dorothy Sayers, or
Charles Williams became well known for their writings, and there
were more than a few who became widely recognized within a spe-
cialized field of study. J. R. R. Tolkien was destined to become the
most famous friend Lewis had, though presentiment could hardly
have gauged the magnitude of popularity for* The Lord of the Rings.
*It seems the most famous person ever to meet with Lewis was evan-
gelist Billy Graham. Graham met Lewis in 1955 while at Cambridge
for a mission to students. Rev. Burton K. Janes, former associate editor of* The Canadian C. S. Lewis Journal, *tells the story.*

In 1979 I read a delightful little book, *Getting Into Print* by
Sherwood E. Wirt with Ruth McKinney (Nashville: Thomas
Nelson, 1977). I especially enjoyed the transcript of Wirt's interview
with C. S. Lewis on May 7, 1963.[1] Lewis spoke incisively on many
topics, including writing, his conversion, encountering Jesus Christ,
modern culture, space travel, and discipline in the Christian life.

Well into the interview, Wirt asked Lewis, "Do you approve of
men such as Bryan Green and Billy Graham asking people to come

144

to a point of decision regarding the Christian life?" Lewis
answered, "I had the pleasure of meeting Billy Graham once. We
had dinner together during his visit to Cambridge University in
1955 while he was conducting a mission to students. I thought he
was a very modest and a very sensible man, and I liked him very
much indeed" (p. 116).

I often wondered about Graham's own version of his meeting
with Lewis—missing from the Graham biographies I had read—
and so took steps to find out. Graham's authorized biographer, the
Reverend John Pollock, assured me that Wirt's quotation could be
treated as authentic, as Graham indeed had lunch with Lewis during his Cambridge Mission, which ran from November 6 to 13,
1955. Pollock reports that Graham "had long admired Lewis and
looked forward to getting to know him. They met at lunch, and
Billy found him to be very kind, gracious, and genial. Lewis said to
Graham, 'You know you have many critics, but I have never met
one of your critics who knows you personally.'"[2]

Wirt himself recalls that a luncheon was arranged at which
Graham met and was seated beside Lewis. Graham, commenting on
a book written about Lewis, *Different Gospels*, later wrote, "I vividly
remember having lunch with him in Cambridge during one of my
several visits to that university where he was professor. I went,
frankly, with some trepidation; what could I possibly say to someone
of such rare genius? And yet he made me feel at ease the moment we
met. My overwhelming memory is that he was one of the most gen-
uinely humble and unassuming men I have ever met. The gospel's
truth clearly had touched not only his mind but his heart and life—
as it must with all who truly follow Christ."[3] (Graham's account is
also told in his memoirs *Just As I Am* on p. 258.)

Returning to Wirt's original question to Lewis, the latter continued, "In a civilization like ours, I feel everyone has to come to terms
with the claims of Jesus Christ upon his life, or else be guilty of in-
attention or of evading the question. In the Soviet Union it is different. Many people living in Russia today have never had to consider
the claims of Christ because they have never heard of those claims."

"In the same way we who live in English-speaking countries have never really been forced to consider the claims, let us say, of Hinduism. But in our Western civilization we are obligated both morally and intellectually to come to grips with Jesus Christ; if we refuse to do so we are guilty of being bad philosophers and bad thinkers"(p. 117).

BOB JONES JR.

Bob Jones University, originally located in College Point, Florida, before moving to Cleveland, Tennessee, and thereafter to Greenville, South Carolina, is an institution known for its clean living and strict rules. It was founded by Bob Jones Sr. as a conservative Christian school with high standards. Cigarettes, chewing tobacco, and alcoholic beverages are among the many things eschewed by the institution. Bob Jones Jr., son of the school's founder, met with C. S. Lewis while visiting England after World War II. Burton K. Janes gives an account of the visit.

The meeting of Bob Jones Jr. (1911–1997), self-described as "an outspoken fundamentalist," with C. S. Lewis is documented elsewhere.[4] Walter Hooper, who met Jones in 1954, asked him what he thought of Lewis. A severe look crossed Jones's face, "That man smokes a pipe," he slowly answered, "and that man drinks liquor," he added, then after a pause said, "but I *do* believe he is a Christian." Jones's own recollection in recent years of his meeting with Lewis carries with it a strong lesson in tolerance and acceptance, and an attempt to understand an individual of a different theological persuasion.

Shortly after the Second World War, Jones and the Anglican bishop, the Reverend A. W. Goodman Hudson, were passing through Oxford. Lewis and Goodman Hudson had been associated in some special activity during the war. Through Goodman Hudson, Jones met Lewis, who came to lunch with them at the hotel there, either the Mitre or the public house, The Eagle and Child (popularly called "The Bird and Baby").

While the trio was eating, Lewis drank about a pint of ale and smoked his pipe. "Of course," Jones wrote a correspondent in 1979, "it is very difficult for me to reconcile the pipe and the tankard of ale with a Christian testimony."

During their meal, Lewis spoke of his conversion. Then he expressed keen interest in the philosophical implications of how God answers prayer, a subject which led to a lengthy discussion, although in 1994 Jones could recall none of the details. Lewis also discussed the book—on prayer—that he was planning to write. Was it the same idea that came to fruition nearly two decades later as *Letters to Malcolm: Chiefly on Prayer*?

Following lunch, Lewis pushed his chair back and re-lit his pipe. "Which of my books do you like the best?" he asked Jones.

Rather apologetically, Jones said that Lewis's trilogy—*Out of the Silent Planet, Perelandra (Voyage to Venus)* and *That Hideous Strength*—which he thought posed theological problems under the guise of science fiction, appealed to him more than anything else Lewis had written.

Clapping his hands, Lewis said, "Good show! Those are my own favorites."

Thirty-one years old, Jones had been tremendously impressed with *The Screwtape Letters* when it appeared in 1942. In the years after their meeting, Jones read more of Lewis's works and saw *Shadowlands* a couple of times.[5]

"Lewis may not always have been orthodox," Jones commented in his autobiography, "but he was seldom dull." While he admitted that his own impression of Lewis continued to be ambivalent, he identified him as a very interesting writer because he "seemed to be especially gifted at making theology simple and setting forth theological truths in allegorical form. . . ." Among the reams of material written about Lewis since his death in 1963, Jones felt that "the 'New Evangelicals' seem to have embraced him as sort of a patron saint, and fundamentalists generally seem to shy away from him as a heretic." However, he concluded, "in conversation, he gave a very good personal testimony of his own faith in Christ."

Hooper thinks that the teetotaler Jones "learned something very valuable about the behavior of not just one fellow Christian, but most of them. And it certainly had not led him to be bitter." That perhaps the most uncompromising fundamentalist in America at that time could meet the unconventional, broadminded Anglican Lewis and accept him as fellow believer gives hope to those of us who pray ardently for spiritual unity among believers if organic unity is not attainable. Any progress along these lines would serve to demolish what Lewis called "our tragic and sinful divisions" and replace them with a certain heavenly unity.[6]

The Eagle and Child, a.k.a. The Bird and Baby pub, where Lewis frequently met with friends.

BITS
AND PIECES

The following bits and pieces were published over the years in The
Canadian C. S. Lewis Journal.

*The internationally renowned Canadian novelist Robertson Davies
(1913–95) was a student at Balliol College, Oxford, in the late
1930s. Years later, as the Master of Massey College in the University
of Toronto, he wrote this letter to Stephen Schofield, subscribing to*
The Canadian C. S. Lewis Journal.

> January 22, 1979
> Dear Sirs:
> I enclose a cheque for a subscription to the
> Journal. During my time at Oxford I attended lec-
> tures by Lewis and admired him greatly and am
> pleased that a Journal to celebrate his fame has
> been founded in Canada.
> > Yours Sincerely,
> > Robertson Davies
> > Toronto

I don't think I heard C. S. Lewis deliver any lectures. Indeed, I'm sure I didn't, for that is something I would have remembered. My father, Professor C. J. Sisson was Pro-Provost of University College, London, at Aberystwyth (not Bangor) and C. S. Lewis stayed one night with us. He was very kind to me as an ignorant young student and he recommended to me the books of Tolkien, starting with *The Hobbit.* I promised to read it, but, of course, never would have bothered, except that, bless him! he sent me an inscribed copy as soon as he returned to Oxford. It remains one of my most treasured possessions—as is the memory of that firelit evening in Aberystwyth in 1942.

—Rosemary Anne Sisson
London

I just heard of a Lewis incident on Radio 4 (7.15, 25/11/89). Apparently C. S. Lewis was travelling on a train one day, shabbily attired as usual, in a first-class compartment, when a rather superior lady came in and after one look at him, she enquired, "Are you sure you have a first-class ticket?" "Yes," replied Lewis, "but I'm afraid I shall need it for myself."

—Peter Brierley
Bromley, Kent

Josephina de Vasconcellos is an accomplished sculptor whose many creations and activities are listed in Who's Who. Among her many honors is the MBE, awarded to her in 1985. The daughter of H. H. de Vasconcellos, Brazilian Consul-General in England, and Freda Coleman, she married the painter Delmar Banner (deceased, 1983) in 1930, and in her 90s remains busy at work on her sculptures. She and her husband met with Lewis on several occasions and exchanged a few letters.

The first time my husband and I met Lewis (after various correspondence) in his room at Magdalen—Delmar's old college—they did most of the talking. Later, Delmar asked me my impression of the great man. I found him charming, with a very personal warmth of communication. I noticed an odd thing—a mat at the knee place at his desk, shaped as though it had been in a car, with 3 slits! It seemed to me highly symbolic in such a humorous way— looking as though the unseen Hand Brake was most in use. It gave me the idea he was being careful of something to be avoided!

We had several meetings ("Meet me at the Mitred Tap" he once wrote, which was the great place for meeting dons etc. back then) and a few letters between him and Delmar—communication was easy, humorous, with references understood. He was a warm, kind man. . . . He was pleased that of all his books, we liked *Perelandra* the best. He answered [our praise of the book] with, "Cats like being stroked."

> —Josephina de Vasconcellos (Mrs. Delmar Banner)
> Ambleside, Cumbria

I was particularly intrigued by the contributions of Lewis's women pupils. I was actually in her room in 1948 when Helen Gardner over the telephone tried to negotiate "her ten" into tutorials by himself on the metaphysicals, and received implacable refusal, on the grounds that the poets were inappropriately erotic. She appeared vexed and baffled. An authority on John Donne, she was totally impervious to gender problems, and we were privileged to profit from her passion and scrupulous scholarship.

As a commoner out of St. Hilda's (College, Oxford) 1947–50 I attended C. S Lewis on Milton, always in packed halls—as indeed were Lord David Cecil's. I found them of immense encouragement. He came across as a strong, well-centred person with a tremendous range. I think we all regarded him as reflecting his two great themes, heroic and epic, with no trace of sentimentality. Also we heard vague rumours of rambunctious beer-swilling evenings with male cronies, one of whom, Charles Willliams, I think had an unusual "voice," mysterious and unfulfilled.

C. S. Lewis in fact marked our "responsions" and I must have absorbed more than I realised as he granted me an A/b. This perplexed Helen Gardner who had realistically rated me as a middle achiever, and for a term she dubiously tutored me on my own, which pressure I found overwhelming. It is possible that psychologically I felt a natural empathy with his approach, which seemed to me liberating, and I could concentrate fully only within such parameters. That may well be a flight of fancy; now more detached in my sixties, I prefer to pay unreserved tribute to the many dons and fellow undergraduates who enabled appreciation of literature and experiences of life to flower.

It did surprise me that "evangelical" Christian bookshops promote his "religious" books. Exploring that evident fact could provide a universal thesis! *A Grief Observed* however confronts human suffering at its deepest level with both sensitive perception and vigorous honesty, thereby winning a universal response.

Sadly, I have not kept my lecture notes for 1947. But my distinct recollection is that they did follow the format of *A Preface to Paradise Lost* because it was remarked at the time we could have just read the book. Of course we did read it and inwardly digest. But his particular unique grand rolling delivery was a delight in itself. (The text of the book in fact did not echo his own speech rhythms as writing often does.) The Satan lecture really dominated the course—double empathy perhaps.

—Mary Wright
St. Bees

Penelope Fitzgerald is the author of several novels including The Beginning of Spring, The Gate of Angels, The Bookshop: A Novel, *and* The Blue Flower. *She was an undergraduate at Oxford in the pre-war years, attending Lewis's introductory lecture series to medieval and renaissance literature.*

My copy of *The Poetical Works of Spenser* once belonged to my mother, who took it with her to Oxford as a student in 1904. On the flyleaf are my own Oxford notes in faded pencil: "C. S. L. says forget courtly Spenser dreamy Spenser—think of rustic Spenser English Spenser homely Spenser, kindled lust, worldy muck, bag-pipes, goat-milking."

It calls up the sight and sound of the lecture room with C. S. Lewis, darkly red-faced and black-gowned, advancing toward the platform—talking already, for he saved time by beginning just inside the door. The place was always crowded, often with a row of nuns at the back. His eye was on all of us: "I shall adapt myself to the slowest note-taker among you."

I was at Somerville College from 1935 to 1938. Although Lewis, opening his stores of classical and medieval learning, said that he was only telling us what we could very well find out for ourselves, we were truly thankful for what we received. Connoisseurs may have preferred the scarcely audible lectures of the poet Edmund Blunden, given in much smaller room. But Lewis was the indis-pensable teacher, about whom all we personally knew was that he was pipe- and beer-loving, lived outside Oxford and made a "thing" of disliking the twentieth century: when T. S. Eliot came to read "The Waste Land" to the Poetry Society, Lewis was not there. Although I don't like Lewis's theology or his politics, his marvelous lectures impressed me at the time as they did everyone who heard them—they made us see Chaucer & Spenser in a totally different light and they influenced me not only during my final exams but even to this day.

—Penelope Fitzgerald
London

C. S. Lewis with his brother and best friend, Warren, on the east coast of Ireland in 1949. They were both quite fond of the sea.

NOTES

Chapter 3, "Narnia: The Domain of Lewis's Beliefs"

1. Professor Manzalaoui notes, "The term '*strict* allegory' I take from Dr. Richard Purtill of Western Washington—I wish to acknowledge a debt to him which he would recognize here and elsewhere in this essay."

2. This book's editor thinks the treatment of the Dufflepuds *is* fair, being amusing and humorous rather than calloused.

3. The editor again disagrees with Professor Manzalaoui, finding it hard to see how someone can claim that Lewis is treating a *fictitious* religion unfairly. The Calormene god Tash is a creation of Lewis's, and as a creation, he may ascribe whatever qualities he desires to the god and the religion surrounding him. Yet even if this religion does have some components of Islam reflected in its credo, the comparison is not unjust. Islam does formally speak of Allah as being compassionate and merciful, yet the phrase "irresistible and inexorable" comes closer to how he is portrayed and truly perceived in the Muslim world. This is also true for many of the Hindu and aboriginal deities worshiped around the globe—emphasis remains more on "appeasing" the gods than ascribing any saving characteristics such as compassion or mercy to their good graces.

4. Professor Manzalaoui has a notion that the Narnian lamppost was inspired by a Victorian gas lamppost which stands alone in a field surrounded by trees in Newnham, Cambridge. It was placed there by the residents of Newnham in the nineteenth century to give light for nighttime skating when the nearby River Cam

overflowed onto the field and the water froze. As the Newnham lamppost had some measure of renown, Manzalaoui speculates that Lewis might have been aware of its existence and used that visual imagery in his fictional lamppost that stood in the woods connecting Professor Kirke's wardrobe to Narnia. Kathryn Lindskoog comments further on this in the appendix to her book *Journey into Narnia.*

5. In fact, it was this very feature of myth mixing that made these books unpalatable to J. R. R. Tolkien. He thought *The Lion, the Witch, and the Wardrobe*, for example, almost worthless. It seemed like a jumble of unrelated mythologies to him, effecting a painfully incongruous reading experience. To put Aslan, the fauns, the White Witch, Father Christmas, the nymphs, Mr. and Mrs. Beaver and the like—all of which had distinct mythological or imaginative origins—into a single imaginative country seemed like a terrible mistake.

6. Contrary to A. N. Wilson's view in his *C. S. Lewis: A Biography* (cf. pages 228–30), Susan's sin was not that of "growing up." Her sin was that of *disbelief*, acquired as she grew older. As Lady Polly points out in *The Last Battle*, Susan's downfall came because she *didn't* grow up.

7. Professor Manzalaoui writes, "When Lewis was writing his Narnia books, he had recently had a student writing a B. Litt. thesis under him on eighteenth-century English translations from Arabic. This no doubt led the conscientious supervisor to reread the *Arabian Nights*, the book of tales which has contributed so strongly to the background of *The Horse and His Boy*. The student himself came from that same background, but Lewis possibly noticed that he was attending the meetings, which Lewis presided over, of the Socratic Club, a society for the rational discussion of the Christian religion. Perhaps he also noticed him at some of the public religious addresses that he gave. Just possibly, that is how, and in part only, of course, the character of Emeth took shape. And, as you will by now have guessed, I wonder if the flattering portrayal of Emeth is a Narnian transformation of myself."

Chapter 4, "C. S. Lewis and God's Surprises"

1. "The Humanitarian Theory of Punishment" can be found in the book of Lewis essays entitled *God in the Dock.*

Chapter 6, "Forty Years' Perspective"

1. On pages 9 and 12 of the Winter 1984 issue of *The Canadian C. S. Lewis Journal*, Fryer had quoted a long passage from *The Historic Faith*, first published in 1883 by B. F. Westcott, Regius Professor of Divinity in Cambridge and Bishop of Durham. In part, it read, "Two thoughts bearing upon the future find clear expression in the New Testament. The one is the consequences of unrepented sin . . . . We read of a sin which has no forgiveness in this world, nor in the world to come; and on the other side, we read of the purpose, the good pleasures of God, through Christ to reconcile all things unto Himself, whether things upon earth or things in the Heavens; of the restitution of all things; of the bringing to naught of the last enemy, Death, and the final subjection of all things to God. . . . If we are called upon to decide which of these two thoughts of Scripture must be held to prevail, we can hardly doubt that that which is the most comprehensive—that which reaches the farthest, contains the ruling idea; and that is the idea of a final, Divine, unity . . . ."

Chapter 7, "I Sleep but My Heart Watcheth"

1. Martin Moynihan notes, "It was from a lecture by R. G. Collingwood that I learned that Realism was the medieval word for Idealism with, for opposite, nominalism. And see *The Magdalen Metaphysicals*, by James Patrick. Thoughts are as real as things; the intellectual and spiritual worlds are real as matter apprehended by the senses."

2. Lewis was referring to Romans 13:1.

3. *Letters: C. S. Lewis, Don Giovanni Calabria: A Study in Friendship.* Translated and edited by Martin Moynihan. London: Collins, 1988.

4. *Te beatum dico et dicam* is rendered in English as "I call you blessed and always shall."

5. Song of Songs 5:2, "I sleep, but my heart waketh: it is the voice of my beloved that knocketh, saying, Open to me, my sister, my love, my dove, my undefiled: for my head is filled with dew, and my locks with the drops of the night" (KJV).

Chapter 9, "Courtesy and Learning"

1. First appearing in *The Canadian C. S. Lewis Journal* and later reprinted in chapter 7 of *In Search of C. S. Lewis.*

Chapter 10, "Wartime Tutor"

1. While probably not the "world's greatest authority" on this matter, Warren Lewis was certainly well informed about this period of French history. In fact, he wound up publishing seven books of seventeenth/eighteenth century French history and biography.

Chapter 12, "Awe and Delight"

1. Rosamund Cowan had written of her tutorials with Lewis, "It was a joy to study with Lewis. He treated us like queens."

Chapter 14, "Uncrowned King of Oxford"

1. Peter Kreeft's book *Between Heaven and Hell* (InterVarsity Press) grew out of this occurrence. It is an imaginary dialogue between Lewis, Kennedy, and Huxley that takes place in post-death limbo, representing "The Great Conversation" that has gone on for millennia between ancient Western theism (Lewis's stance), modern Western humanism (Kennedy's position), and ancient Eastern Pantheism (championed by Huxley).

2. These statements agree with others made by those who knew Lewis—he was opinionated, yet open to new findings, capable of surprising and being surprised. This contrasts with the dubious pronouncements made by A. N. Wilson in his Lewis biography, who accused Lewis of avoiding challenging ideas and allowing "a carapace of intellectual laziness" to harden upon him (cf. *C. S. Lewis: A Biography*, p. 162).

Chapter 17, "Shadowlands"

1. Letter of Sheldon Vanauken to the editor.

Chapter 18, "The Schoolboy Johnson"

1. After Lindskoog's book was published, *The Canadian C. S. Lewis Journal* editor Stephen Schofield spent the next four years gathering evidence to refute Lindskoog's claim that C. S. Lewis did not write the unfinished science fiction piece called *The Dark Tower*. In addition to firsthand inspection of the manuscript, Schofield hired several handwriting experts to compare the handwriting of *The Dark Tower* manuscript with other Lewis texts. Independently, they unanimously concluded that C. S. Lewis was indeed the author of *The Dark Tower*. By the end of 1992 the mat-

ter was settled, as evidence for Lewis authenticity was overwhelming, including the admission by Lindskoog that she herself had committed forgery in writing spurious letters to support her claims.

Chapter 19, "C. S. Lewis and Adultery"

1. In his book (p. 131), Wilson stated (without listing any source for his presumption), "The idea of the evening was primarily to get drunk, and this was a matter about which Lewis was exuberantly insistent." By way of response, Norman Bradshaw, a former pupil of Lewis who—unlike Wilson—actually attended these get-togethers, wrote to Stephen Schofield, saying, "At the 'Schools' Dinners (parties for those who had just finished final exams), there was certainly no encouragement of 'dirty stories and drunkenness.' The 'beer and Beowulf' evenings I have little recollection of—except being *bored* stiff. A certain amount of drinking was expected . . . and anything that lowered sex from romance to the animal level was delighted in (he was afraid that love could become idolatry) but I never found 'dirty stories' *encouraged*. The masculine society of a 'club' or 'mess-room' he found congenial and I suppose his parties were modeled on the talk there. . . . I never saw anyone *drunk* at his parties and we never swapped dirty stories." W. R. Fryer, another Lewis pupil at that time, writes, "I am happy to comment on CSL's having allegedly encouraged his undergraduate guests to dirty jokes and drunkenness. All the evidence I have, from my own time [1930s], goes flatly to contradict these reports. CSL more than once invited Norman and me, together with my historian contemporary, Cyril Gilbey. We much enjoyed these occasions: friendly, easy, flowing with chat and comical give-and-take, tobacco smoke and beer. The great man did not encourage dirty jokes or taking too much to drink. I suspect that those who now write about CSL, never having met him, may all too probably take far too nearly at face value tales which are told about Lewis by older men who did know him, or knew others who had really known him, and that these tales had grown higher in each telling."

2. Wilson had also written (on p. 131), "The conversation had to be what he called 'bawdry.' 'Nothing above the belly or below the knee tonight!' he exclaimed on one of these evenings, savouring the rowdy songs and bawdy rhymes which resulted." Wilson

goes on to take statements of a former Lewis pupil, Roger Lancelyn Green, out of context (a recurring fault in Wilson's assessments) as proof that Lewis enjoyed 'drunken all-male "stag" evenings' of coarse talk. But the Green passage that Wilson quotes actually says the *opposite*, namely that "By 'bawdy,' Lewis did not mean what are commonly called dirty stories. He disliked stories containing smut or that bordered upon the blasphemous and, when told in his presence, he did not disguise his annoyance.' By his own definition, bawdy ought to be outrageous and extravagant, but it must not have anything cruel or pornographic about it." Lewis's own diary—written even before he had become a Christian—shows Wilson's statements are misleading and inaccurate. From the March 1, 1927, entry, Lewis writes about an undergraduate society called the Mermaids, who met together for the purpose of reading and discussing literature, "I am entertaining the Mermaids tonight, drat 'em. They are nothing but a drinking, guffawing cry of barbarians with hardly any taste among them, and I wish I hadn't joined them: but I don't see my way out now. . . . Back to College, and had to spend most of the time getting things ready for the sons of Belial. The evening passed off all right I think: Tourneur's *Revenger's Tragedy* was read, a rotten piece of work, whose merits, pretty small to begin with, were entirely lost in the continual cackling which greeted every bawdy reference (however tragic) and every mistake made by a reader. If one spent much time with these swine one would blaspheme against humor itself, as being nothing but a kind of shield with which rabble protect themselves from anything that might disturb the muddy puddle inside them."

Chapter 20, "Surprised by *Shadowlands*"

1. This quotation comes from Lewis's sermon "The Weight of Glory."

Chapter 21, "Encounter in a Two-Bit Pub"

1. Lewis's account of Joy's recovery is told in "The Efficacy of Prayer," which appeared in the January 1959 issue of *The Atlantic Monthly*, later reprinted in *The World's Last Night and Other Essays*. While recovery from untreated cancer metastasis is exceptional, there are other people besides Joy Lewis who have experienced this phenomenon. See, for example, Tilden Everson and Warren Coles's

classic study of 176 cases entitled *Spontaneous Regression of Cancer*, published in 1966. For a fascinating discussion of others who have experienced the rare spontaneous remission from cancer, read Caryle Hirshberg and Marc Ian Barasch's intriguing book *Remarkable Recovery*, released in 1995.

2. "Carol" was Dr. Morris's first wife, an invalid for much of their marriage before she died.

3. Matthew 15:21–28

4. Luke 16:1–15

Chapter 24, "Reminiscenses of the Oxford Lewis"

1. Many books of Lewis biography or works about his literary achievements have been written by Americans (an example of the former being *C. S. Lewis: Images of His World* by Douglas Gilbert/Clyde Kilby, while Paul Ford's *The Companion to Narnia* demonstrates the latter); and many English folks who have contributed their reminiscences of Lewis have done so because of the promptings and requests from Americans, such as *C. S. Lewis at the Breakfast Table*, a compendium of memoirs mostly written by English denizens at the behest of *The New York C. S. Lewis Society*, edited by American James T. Como.

2. A "starets" is a spiritual advisor or religious teacher in the Eastern Orthodox Church. A starets is not necessarily a priest, but someone recognized for his piety, to whom both monks and members of the laity alike turn for spiritual guidance.

3. Lewis had a long discussion about metaphor, myth and Christianity with both Hugo Dyson and J. R. R. Tolkien that started on the evening of September 19, 1931, and continued on into the early hours of the next morning. Within two weeks, Lewis was able to write to Arthur Greeves that "I have just passed on from believing in God to definitely believing in Christ—in Christianity."

4. Sheldon and Jean "Davy" Vanauken were Americans living in Oxford in the early 1950s while Sheldon was doing graduate work at Jesus College. Their marriage was celebrated years later in *A Severe Mercy*.

5. Probably the closest he came to this sort of disclosure in print was his posthumous *Letters to Malcolm: Chiefly on Prayer*.

6. Professor Taylor opposed Lewis on religious grounds, but they got along quite well on other fronts, walking together—for

example—round Addison's walk, swimming in the Cherwell River, and discussing literature and history. See chapter 15 of Stephen Schofield's *In Search of C. S. Lewis.*

7. Although Mrs. Moore could be demanding of Lewis's time, she and her daughter Maureen also brought a domestic comfort to Lewis's life that greatly broadened his social experience. Indeed, much of Lewis's insight into human nature came from the people he met through his association with Mrs. Moore. While in the later years of Mrs. Moore's life (she died in 1951) Lewis did show a great deal of charity towards her increasingly senile behavior, their coming to live together three decades earlier in the 1920s was mutually agreeable, not something done out of sympathy on Lewis's part.

Chapter 25, "Sightings"
Billy Graham

1. Also printed in *Decision*, September and October 1963; and *God in the Dock*, ed. Walter Hooper (Grand Rapids: Eerdmans, 1970).

2. Pollock to Janes, May 10, 1994.

3. Cited by Stephanie Willis, secretary to Billy Graham, to Janes, May 25, 1994.

Bob Jones Jr.

4. Bob Jones Jr., *Cornbread and Caviar* (Greenville, S.C.: Bob Jones University Press, 1985), 66; Roger Lancelyn Green and Walter Hooper, *C. S. Lewis: A Biography* (London: Collins, 1974), 229; Walter Hooper, "C. S. Lewis and C. S. Lewises," in Michael H. Macdonald and Andrew A. Tadie, eds., *G. K. Chesterton and C. S. Lewis: The Riddle of Joy* (Grand Rapids: Eerdmans, 1989), 41; and idem, "C. S. Lewis: The Man and His Thought," in Cynthia Marshal, ed., *Essays on C. S. Lewis and George MacDonald* (Lewiston, N.Y.: Edwin Mellen, 1991), 11.

5. Jones to Janes, November 10, 1993.

6. C. S. Lewis, *Christian Reunion and Other Essays,* ed. Walter Hooper (London: Collins, 1990), 17, 21.